BUILD

MW00736941

CITIES

OF

REFUGE

PREPARING CITIES THROUGH 24/7 WORSHIP FOR THE COMING SYSTEMIC COLLAPSE

Building Cities of Refuge

This book contains sober warnings that make us tremble. More than that, though, it carries a message of hope regarding our Father's plans for the climactic conclusion of natural history. Since this book comes to us from a godly man of prayer, I urge you to read it carefully and prayerfully.

Bob Sorge, author, bobsorge.com

Building Cities of Refuge – Preparing Cities though 24/7 worship for the Coming Systemic Collapse

Copyright c 2013 *by Brondon Mathis*

Cover design by Brondon Mathis

ISBN- 978-0615818573

Printed in the United States of America.

Contact info:
Brondon Mathis
614 467-0165, office
614-745-9683
Brondonnoe4@aol.com
facebook/brondonmathis.com

TABLE OF CONTENTS

INTRODUCTION

HOW TO THRIVE NOT JUST SURVIVE IN THE DAY OF THE LORD

"Building Cities of Refuge" is a book on how the church will be positioned during the unique dynamics surrounding the coming *"Great and Terrible day of the Lord,"* to thrive, not just survive, during the most difficult times in all of Human History. The mandate and revelation for this book was given to me on November 11, 2011, (11-11-11.) It was on this date in Detroit Michigan at *"THE CALL" – Detroit - a 24hr prayer gathering of 40,000 people at Ford Field -* that I was visited by the spirit of God at 3:00 am in the morning with this message and mandate. During this time I was given several messages during a divine visitation from the Lord, that I was mandated to write and put in books, for a time to come. This book is one of a series of books I've currently published on www.Amazon.com from this visitation from the Lord, on 11-11-11.

In this visitation I was given a prophetic word of wisdom for the coming years of 2012-2015, to prepare my heart, life and family for difficult times that are on the horizon in our nation and world. I later realized that it was not just for me and my home, but that it was also a word that I was to begin sharing with the whole body of Christ, helping to prepare the Church for these hard times to come. In this visitation God began to reveal to me what to do to be covered, protected, and provided for supernaturally, during systemic shakings, race riots, and so-called *"Natural disasters,"* coming in the earth as a result of the judgments of God coming on our nation and it's systems in the days to come. Many in the body of Christ believed and prophesied that 2011 would begin these coming judgments of shakings, demonic assaults, unusual weather patterns and racial disturbances, causing economic, financial and relational shakings because of the prophetic significance of this year of 2011.

The Prophetic Symbolism of 2011

The number 11 in numerology means, chaos, disorder, and judgment. The number 11 three times on the Gregorian calendar only comes once in a hundred years. Many prophetic voices had prophesied that 11 three times on the Gregorian calendar in the day, month, and year, could signal the release of judgment, chaos and disorder in our society. This 24hr prayer meeting in Detroit, on November 11, 2011, was focused on how to turn or lessen this judgment on our nation here in the United States, by praying in accordance with Joel 2, in Detroit Michigan, one of the most racially divided and economically depressed cities in the United States. Based on what was revealed to me to prepare my own life, family and City in this visitation at 3:00am in the morning, and what we've seen happening in our nation since that time, I believe 2012 could have possibly began the birth pangs and the forerunner of what's coming in what the bible calls *"The Great and Terrible Day of the Lord,"* and the *CALL DETROIT* was a prescription of how the body of Christ is to respond – *with 24 hr Prayer Vigils* - during coming relational, economic and financial shakings that challenge the infrastructures of cities throughout the nations of the world.

The Drought and the Trayvon Martin Tragedy of 2012 and Financial Collapse of Detroit of 2013

We now know that during the time of the writing of this second book from that visitation, that the following winter of 2012 began a succession of racial conflicts, protests and riots, beginning with the Trayvon Martin killing by a neighborhood watch volunteer,

George Zimmerman, that touched off racial protests, a subsequent murder conviction, trial and a not guilty verdict that exposed the racial divide in our country and set back race relations to 1960's type proportions.

Then in the summer of 2012 was the worst drought to hit the United States of America in over 100 years. This drought was precipitated by temperatures of 110 degrees throughout the country, and began an extended drought in California that touched off wild fires and destroyed properties all up the West Coast.

We also now know that the City of Detroit, in 2013, became the first major city in U.S. History to file for Bankruptcy. Below is an excerpt from www.CBSnews.com

> *Once the very symbol of American industrial might, Detroit became the biggest U.S. city to file for bankruptcy Thursday, its finances ravaged and its neighborhoods hollowed out by a long, slow decline in population and auto manufacturing.*
>
> *The filing, which had been feared for months, put the city on an uncertain course that could mean laying off municipal employees, selling off assets, raising fees and scaling back basic services such as trash collection and snow plowing, which have already been slashed.*
>
> *The result is a city where whole neighborhoods are practically deserted and basic services cut off in places. Looming over the crumbling landscape is a budget deficit believed to be more than $380 million and long-term debt that could be as much as $20 billion.*

The Spirit of the Lord had been revealing to me for several decades, since 1992, that our society and economic system (a debtor society) was headed in our nation for a complete economic and financial collapse. I believe this economic fallout in Detroit in 2013 could be a harbinger of what's coming on a national level, and could be precipitated both by a total financial collapse from out of control debt, and by drought-like weather conditions in this nation and the nations of the earth.

In this visitation I saw these tragic relational racial conflicts, economic and natural disasters escalating over a 3 to 5 year period. In one of the other books I've written from this visitation, *"My Money is Restored,"* I shared what we must do to prepare financially. In this book I want to share what we must do to prepare spiritually in the body of Christ, to come together across denominational and racial lines in key cities around this nation, to establish Cities of Refuge, complete with 24/7 houses of worship and prayer, and storehouses of food, for believers to look to God and one another for sustenance, supply and spiritual and natural food, during this coming larger racial, economic, financial and food fallout in 2015 and beyond. The body of Christ will need to be purified and cleansed to return to **Acts 4 Communities** where we have all things in common and there is none that lack among us.

> *Act 4:31 **And when they had prayed, the place was shaken where they were assembled together;** and they were all filled with the Holy Ghost, and they spake the word of God with boldness. 32 And the multitude of them that believed were of one heart and of one soul: neither said any of them that ought of the things which he possessed was his own; but they had all things common. 33. And with great power gave the apostles witness of the resurrection of the Lord Jesus: and great grace was*

8

upon them all. **34.** **Neither was there any among them that lacked: for as many as were possessors of lands or houses sold them, and brought the prices of the things that were sold, 35 And laid them down at the apostles' feet: and distribution was made unto every man according as he had need.**

CHAPTER 1

THE COMING REVIVAL OF CITY CHURCHES

*Rev 21:9 And there came unto me one of the seven angels which had the seven vials full of the seven last plagues, and talked with me, saying, **Come hither, I will shew thee the bride, the Lamb's wife.** 10 And he carried me away in the spirit to a great and high mountain, <u>and shewed me that great city, the holy Jerusalem, descending out of heaven from God,</u>*

In the 21st century there's a major revival and restoration on the horizon that's going to prepare the Church as a bride adorned for her Husband. In 2012 I believe God shifted His Church in preparation for this revival, positioning her for His coming Kingdom in the earth like no other year since the inception of the Church. In this decade God is going to bring forth a new thing in the Church, and the next and last restoration movement of the church is going to culminate in God unfolding, unveiling and revealing himself through the manifestation of the sons of God in the earth. Men and women of God are going to get a fresh vision and revelation of the real Jesus, the real Church he came to build in the earth, and develop a true heart after God's heart and desire for the earth. This release and restoration is going to begin when we truly find out what was really on God's heart when he said in Matthew 16:17 *"Upon this Rock I will build my Church,"* and finally get a revelation of Jesus Christ, untainted by religion or doctrinal, theological biases or presuppositions, and the church He came to establish in the earth.

The New Expression of the Church in the Earth

This is what John saw of the Church, in the book of the revelation of Jesus Christ, when he saw the New Jerusalem coming down out of heaven as a bride adorned for her husband in Revelation 21.

> *Rev 21:9 And there came unto me one of the seven angels which had the seven vials full of the seven last plagues, and talked with me, saying,* **Come hither, I will shew thee the bride, the Lamb's wife.** *10 And he carried me away in the spirit to a great and high mountain, and shewed me that great city, the holy Jerusalem, descending out of heaven from God,*

> *11 Having the glory of God: and her light was like unto a stone most precious, even like a jasper stone, clear as crystal; 12 And had a wall great and high, and had twelve gates, and at the gates twelve angels, and names written thereon, which are the names of the twelve tribes of the children of Israel:*

> *13 On the east three gates; on the north three gates; on the south three gates; and on the west three gates. 14 And the wall of the city had twelve foundations, and in them the names of the twelve apostles of the Lamb.*

The Angel in Revelation 21 showed John a City descending out of Heaven as a bride, as a great city, having the glory of God. This bride speaks of Israel, and the Church. These are the two main personalities in scripture referred to as the Bride – *Israel in the Old Testament and the Church in the New.* John saw that city, as a bride, having a great and high wall, and having twelve gates, and at the gates twelve angels, with the names or personalities of the twelve tribes of the children of Israel. He saw these twelve gates, three on each side of the city, east, north, south, and west. He

12

saw the wall of the city with twelve foundations, and in them the names, or personalities of the twelve apostles of the Lamb. In this city, he saw a tree that had 12 fruit on the tree, and the leaves were for the healing, or reconciling of the races. This revelation of what John saw of the Holy City was actually a revelation of the glorified Church – *Both Jew and Gentile* - that had been purged and prepared, through the fires of the Holy Ghost and *Tribulation* (Luke 12:49), to be a bride without spot, wrinkle or any such thing.

All Night Prayer Vision - God save Our City

One night in 1993 when I was in an all night prayer time in my Dad's little store front Church, I was praying for an outreach I was having in my city. I was praying over and over again, "GOD SAVE OUR CITY," "GOD SAVE OUR CITY." I felt the Lord ask me, "Do you want me to show you what a saved city looks like?" I said, Yes Lord, show me. He said, "Read Revelation 21." I begin reading Revelation 21 till I fell asleep on the altar. As I fell asleep I had a vision of what I was reading.

A Burning City of Light

I saw the most beautiful city I had ever seen. It was bright as the noon day sun. The whole city was full of light. The foundational color that permeated the whole city was GOLD. Then in the dream the spirit took me back to the process of how the city became bright as the noon day sun. Immediately I was back in my City, Columbus Ohio as it presently was. In the city I saw 12 small flickering lights, barely flickering on each side of town, in the midst of darkness all around.

12 Lights to the City – Praying City Churches on Each Side of Town

The closer I got to those lights I could see that those lights were being fueled by small groups of worshipping and praying believers that were singing and falling on their faces praying in 12 small buildings on 4 sides of the city, in the midst of the darkness of the city. As they continued worshipping and praying, these lights began to grow into huge bon fires, burning and illuminating their particular sides of town, the more the believers worshipped and prayed. As they increased and continued their prayer and worship, people began being drawn to these burning fires out of the darkness, and out of religious churches within the city, without anyone saying anything to them. As they came to the light they began to instinctively worship and pray, as they saw the small groups doing it.

12 Gates and Angels to the City

The more they increased their prayer and worship, the more people were drawn to the light. The more people were drawn to their light the larger the light shined. These 12 little buildings began to be sovereignly transformed from little shack-like buildings into the largest buildings I had ever seen, reaching up to the sky around the city, hovering over homes and whole neighborhoods. They were not skyscrapers, but they reached high around the city. Out of each burning fire coming out of each building were these huge Angels that began to dispel the demons that were responsible for the darkness in the city. The more the people worshipped and prayed the larger the fires burned, the brighter the lights shined, the larger the buildings became, and the bigger the Angels over them grew. In the hands of these angels were the largest swords I had ever seen. Each Angel over each burning building faced outward. Every time foreign entities attempted to enter the city, these Angels, being fueled by the worship and the prayers of the growing groups, would wield their swords, and these intruders to the city would be pushed back and scattered out of the city.

The larger these lights and buildings on each side of town grew; they grew into one giant corporate worship and prayer session, illuminating one giant ball of fiery light, lighting up the whole city. It seemed as if these 12 buildings grew to the size of stadiums full of people, illuminating their light until they were one gigantic expression of the Church in the city; people as far as your eye could see in the city, enraptured in light and pure gold.

When I awoke the Lord spoke to my heart and said, *"The 12 little flickering lights are 12 little praying churches of believers that I will raise up in the years to come, 3 on each side of the town, as Gates and gatekeepers to the city, with power and authority in their prayers to offer up to the King of the City a worthy Bride for His Son."* These 12 praying churches will have angels that will be the gate keepers of the city, teaching and leading the people in prayer and worship. These Gatekeepers will be Apostolic Prophets with the Heart of God that will decree and declare as watchmen, the Will and Word of God over a city. As I awoke and heard God's interpretation of the dream, immediately a verse of scripture dropped into my heart concerning a dream Jacob had about the Church from Genesis 28:17

> *And he was afraid, and said, How dreadful is this place! This is none other than the house of God, AND THIS IS THE GATE OF HEAVEN*

Upon This Rock I Will Build My Church

Our generation has chosen to build His church upon a man's doctrine, or a man's gift, charisma or administrative abilities, rather than on the revelation of Jesus Christ. Therefore we have built organizations, and man-made structures, and we call it His Church, instead of building Holy Cities where He can come and dwell and set up His abode. In the early Church, the Church was all the believers in a city that would meet daily in houses all over the city, and in the Temple for temple prayer. Until we get back to building on the revelation of Jesus Christ we will not build cities where people can encounter and see God, but organizations where people encounter and see a man and his gift, or charisma, along with all of his limitations and shortcomings. This book is a heavenly blueprint, given by the Spirit of wisdom and revelation, for what God intended for His Church, established on a rock, for the building of Holy Cities in the earth known as Cities of Refuge, in preparation for the coming Great and Terrible day of the Lord. This wisdom and revelation of the Church as a City of Refuge will assist the Church in maneuvering through the unique dynamics of the end times, soon to come, as everything in the earth that can be shaken is shaken. But what is that revelation? And where is that revelation found?

> *And I say also unto thee, that thou art Peter, and upon this rock I will build my church and the gates of hell will not prevail against it. (Matt 16:18)*

Before the Lord returns, what the church has been called to become and what the church has been called to do in accomplishing the will of the father in the earth will be restored to her DNA, and take center stage as she's prepared as a bride is prepared when she is being adorned for her husband. At the inception of the church, when Jesus first mentions his intention to build His church in Matthew 16, Jesus gives us His purpose for His church. Jesus asked His Disciples in Matt 16:13

> *Whom do men say that I the Son of man am? 14 And they said, Some say that thou art John the*

16

Baptist: some, Elias; and others, Jeremias, or one of the prophets. 15 He saith unto them, But whom say ye that I am? 16 And Simon Peter answered and said, Thou art the Christ, the Son of the living God. 17 And Jesus answered and said unto him, Blessed art thou, Simon Barjona: for flesh and blood hath not revealed it unto thee, but my Father which is in heaven. 18 And I say also unto thee, that thou art Peter, and upon this rock I will build my church and the gates of hell will not prevail against it. <u>*And I will give unto you the keys to the kingdom of Heaven, and whatever you bind on earth shall be bound in heaven and whatever you loose on earth will be loosed in heaven'*</u> *(*Matt 16:19)

The original purpose of the church was not to hide out in the earth until Jesus returned. The original purpose of the church was not just for believers to come together to have church services. There are three main purposes of the church from these verses in Matthew 16:13-19, that Jesus meant for His church to be established upon.

#1 The Church was to be built upon the Revelation of Jesus Christ - *Thou art the Christ, the Son of the Living God.* v.16

#2 The Church was built for battle - *The gates of hell will not prevail against it.* v. 18

#3 The Church was to be built upon Prayer, to bind the kingdom of darkness, and to release heaven on earth - *And whatever you bind on earth shall be bound in heaven... whatever you loose on earth will be loosed in heaven.* v. 19

17

The main purpose of the church was that through prayer and the worship of Jesus as (Messiah) King of the whole earth, we would call forth; "*Thy kingdom come, Thy will be done, in earth as it is in heaven* (Mat. 6:10). I believe this is the rock, that if the Church would be built upon – *1) A Revelation of Jesus; 2) A Battle Plan; and 3) A Place of Prayer* – she would bring forth the kingdom of God in the earth, establishing Cities of God's glory and presence in the earth, as it is in heaven. I believe these keys given to His church are the same keys that were given to David – *the keys of the Tabernacle of David* - to establish the throne and the kingdom that the messiah would sit upon (Isaiah 22:22, Amos 9:11, Rev. 3:7), a kingdom of unceasing and incessant worship and prayer to Jesus, (Ps. 72) the king of the whole earth, which would release revelation in the earth of Jesus and the Kingdom of Heaven. These keys would open the windows of heaven for the ascending and descending of angels, and shut the gates to the Kingdom of darkness, to prohibit the unlawful ascending and descending in the heavens and earth of Satan and His demons.

Within this original mission statement of the church, recorded in Matthew 16-16-19, it is prophesied that the gates of hell would (*assail against the church*), but would not be able to prevail against it. This is a prophecy of a conflict between the kingdom of darkness and the Kingdom of Heaven. The Church was to be built for battle, and that battle would only be undertaken victoriously by the church established upon *THE REVELATION OF JESUS, THE CHRIST that would produce unceasing and incessant worship of this man as the King of the nations.* Only the church that would be built upon this revelation would be considered His Church - *the Church of Jesus Christ.* Only the church built upon this revelation would be capable of being transformed to become what Jesus said we'd become and to do what Jesus said we would do. What is it going to take to get the church back to what Jesus envisioned when he founded her upon His very own revelation? She must return to her original purpose. What is it going to take to return

18

her back to her place of practice, presence and power in the earth? To return to what Jesus intended for his church we're going to have to understand and embrace the revelation of Jesus Christ. What is it? What does the revelation of Jesus Christ look like in practical terms? Because if we just stop at getting *"A Revelation of Jesus Christ,"* we usually end up in so broad of terms that every denomination would instantly refer to their denominational doctrine and revelation of what they emphasize of who Jesus is as related to what Jesus supposedly revealed to their leader or founder.

The Rock of the Church

When I refer to the revelation of Jesus Christ I'm not referring to some man's latest, greatest, mystic doctrinal dogma that binds whole denominations in an elitist, separatist stronghold. I'm not speaking about an abstract mystical thing that can't be grasped or pinpointed by His body at large. Nor am I just speaking about Peter's statement in Matt 16:17 *"thou art the Christ, the son of the living God,"* from a religious, churchy vantage point. What does that really mean *"Thou art the Christ,"* from the Jewish mindset? The Christ speaks of the Messiah who would come as a King and set up again the throne of David and reign as King over all the kingdoms of the earth, overthrowing and dethroning all the kings of the earth hostile to his reign. Therefore, the revelation of Christ in the Jewish mind and the revelation of Christ from the religious church mindset are often two different paradigms. One, the Jewish paradigm of the Church built upon a rock, is speaking of a judicial kingdom established on a throne to be the highest court in the land, establishing justice in the earth for the oppressed through day and night prayer (Luke 18:1-8). The other, the religious paradigm of the Church upon a rock is speaking of a pseudo-spiritual immaterial institution that often times is irrelevant and out of touch with the injustice in the earth, seeking an other-worldly escape from the unjust oppression.

19

The Revelation of Jesus Christ

When the bible speaks of the father's revelation of Jesus as Christ that was revealed to Peter, it's not speaking of something religious, abstract, or mystical, unable to be grasped or understood to us in the 21st century. The Father made sure we would know what that revelation was, because without it the gates of Hell would prevail against the church. Without it the church would not know how to engage the enemy. Without it the church would not know how to bind the unjust kingdom of darkness and bring justice and the righteous kingdom of God to the earth.

The Book of the Revelation of Jesus Christ

This revelation of Jesus as Christ was left in the earth by the Holy Spirit for the church, revealed to Peter at that moment, but further revealed and explained in detail and in all of his glory to the Apostle John on the isle of Patmos. The rock that the church is founded upon is found throughout scripture but culminating in *The Book of the Revelation of Jesus Christ*. Throughout scripture we've received a revelation of Jesus Christ beginning in Genesis, as a microscopic lens that is being adjusted and focused until in the final book of the New Testament, the Book of the Revelation of Jesus Christ, the lens is finally focused and made clear and plain for all to see. It's the book that Jesus revealed to the Church of the glorified Christ and His plan to transition the earth through the unique dynamics at the end of the age, to the establishing of His coming kingdom in the earth. To really grasp the purpose of the church we must return to the mind of God for what Jesus intended for His Church when he established her upon this rock. If we're going to accomplish our mission in the earth we're going to have to go to the end of the book, the book the enemy has had us avoiding for years and years and find our purpose in Christ, and His plan to transition the earth to the new age. We're going to have to go to the book of the Revelation of Jesus Christ and get a vision of the beauty of the Glorified Christ, King of all the earth. It's this revelation that will cause the Church to become a Glorified Church partnering with him for the establishing of his kingdom in the earth.

Once we truly understand this rock that the church was built upon, and get back to it as the very foundation of our existence, the end–time Church will began to change in such a way as to enter into her end-time purpose, that she will not look anything like she has looked over the last one hundred and fifty years or so. The Revelation of Jesus Christ from this book will begin to transform her into what he originally intended for her to look like. As we behold the Beauty of the Lord and get a revelation of Jesus Christ, the Church at the end of the age is going to take on the nature and the character of her Bridegroom, preparing her for the coming day of the Lord.

What a city of refuge is supposed
to look like -
Layout in Revelation
the Holy city
the atmosphere of heaven on earth

~~clear clean~~
An impenetrable city
in which the Darkness can't get in

CHAPTER 2

BUILDING 24/7 HOUSES OF PRAYER IN THE SPIRIT OF THE TABERNACLE OF DAVID

11 On that day I will raise up the Tabernacle of David, which has fallen down, and repair its damages; I will raise up its ruins, and rebuild it as in the days of old... (Amos 9:11)

The church of Jesus Christ is at a very critical time in her existence in the earth. She's at a time where if she doesn't recapture her original purpose and mission her flame is being threatened to be extinguished by the forces of secularism, post modernism and the many secular agendas of our day that are motivated by the forces of darkness arrayed against the church. Before the Lord returns what the church will be and what the church will do in accomplishing the will of the father in the earth will take center stage as she's prepared as a bride adorned for her husband, bringing her back to her original purpose. One of the main components that need to be restored to the church if she is going to withstand the onslaught of the enemy at the end of the age is her original and eternal identity as a house of prayer. At the end of the age God is going to restore his house as a house of prayer, empowering her to accomplish her end-time calling in the earth. For those that will position themselves to be able to give to rebuild and restore His house as a house of prayer God's going to release David type wealth, favor and blessing at the end of the age to the body of Christ.

A New Thing in an Old System

Remember not the former things, neither consider the things of old, Behold I do a New Thing, Now it shall spring forth. Isaiah 43:19.....

I'm Doing a New Thing, but My Church Keeps on Doing the Same Ole Things – (Holy Spirit)

In 1999 as I was praying about the direction of the body of Christ going into a new decade, century and millennium, God spoke to my heart and began to relate to me His heart and vision for the 21st century church. He began to tell me about a church that I had no grid or paradigm for. I heard something that caused me to check whether I was hearing from the right spirit. I heard, *"In the 21st century church is going to be opened like Wal-Mart, 24hrs a day."* I felt like I had heard the spirit saying, the church won't be known by its buildings or it's separate, distinct congregations, but that it would be known by the body of believers in whole cities. At the time I was a new Pastor, leading a traditional apostolic storefront Church of 150 people that my Father had started in 1986 in the inner-city of downtown Columbus Ohio. My father led that church for 11years, when in 1997 he installed me as the Pastor and he became the overseer. From 1997 to 1998 we grew from about 35 people to about 150 people, which was a miracle for a traditional Apostolic Oneness Church. However, in 1999 God spoke a verse of Scripture into my heart from Isaiah 43:18,19 that says, *Remember not the former things, neither consider the things of old, Behold I do a New Thing, Now it shall spring forth.* Then he said these words to me. *Brondon, I'm doing a New Thing, but my Church keeps doing the same ole things.*

24

You must let go of the Old to see the New

I said, "God, tell me how to do this new thing and I'll do it." He said "You won't do it even if I told you!" You were a traditional church goer, who grew up from a traditional church boy, and you're now a traditional church preacher. What the church of this generation has shown you is what you're going to do, even if I tell you to do something different. In order for you to do something new you've got to SEE something new. In order to see something new you've got to LET GO OF THE OLD...*Remember not the former things....BEHOLD, I do a New Thing...(Isa. 43:18,19)*

Hebrews 11:1 says *Faith is the substance of things not seen.* After you let go of the old, (*what you can see*) by faith, you can *BEHOLD, or SEE the new.* He said, "What you are doing now is what the church of this generation has shown you, and told you that you must do to be successful in building a church." However, it's not MY church they've been building. It's been their vain attempts at accomplishment, greatness in their religious circles, fame, and/or worldly success. Today the church you know measures success by how many people are coming. I set the standard of success in my church in the book of Acts by how many people were praying.

> *Act 4:31 And when they had prayed, the place was shaken where they were assembled together; and they were all filled with the Holy Ghost, and they spake the word of God with boldness. 32 And the multitude of them that believed were of one heart and of one soul: neither said any of them that ought of the things which he possessed was his own; but they had all things common.*

As I stated earlier, I had no grid or paradigm for this type of a church. All I could see was that if I was going to get this new paradigm I was definitely going to have to let go of the former thing. He instructed me to shut down the ministry I was heading up in 1999, but I relented. The whole year of 1999 it was a struggle that almost destroyed my marriage and family. Anytime you keep doing something that God tells you not to do, you will continue on to your own demise. Finally at the end of 1999 I resigned as Pastor of Apostolic Deliverance Church and begin to attend another ministry in my city until further notice, waiting for God to reveal to me the Wal-Mart structure for this New Thing. Further notice didn't come until the end of 2007 going into 2008, eight years later. By this time I had accepted a position as a staff Pastor at a Large Multi-ethnic Mega Church in my city, and had been on staff there since 2001. While serving at this Mega-church I had gone from taking a position as the janitor at the church, to being a staff Pastor overseeing their whole Outreach department of over 300 volunteers, as well as preaching about once a month to the congregation that numbered about five thousand.

Things were exploding in my life and ministry. We went on to establish 4 inner-city satellite churches from that ministry, where we saw over 10,000 people saved from all walks of life. We were hosting daily early Morning Prayer meetings at 5am with hundreds of people, and weekly all night prayer meetings every Friday night that was changing the very fabric of our inner city. I was invited several times to the Mayor's office in our city of 1.6 million people to help with our city-wide initiative to curtail crime and lawlessness in the inner-city. Because I had been hosting inner-city tent crusades where whole gangs were being saved and whole projects were being transformed the Police chief had my number and would call me to help them anytime there was a disturbance in these communities. The Mayor offered to give me access to all of the city's recreation centers to turn them into Hope Centers. I was traveling all over the world preaching and telling of what God was doing in bringing revival to our city through our inner-city Outreach ministry. In 2008 while I was still struggling with resigning, a national speaker and intercessor from Kansas City Missouri came to our church to preach and talk about an upcoming Solemn Assembly prayer gathering in Cincinnati Ohio entitled "The Call." It was due to take place later that week. The founder, Lou Engle, was preaching at our church. While preaching he looked down to me sitting on the front row to his right and began speaking to me from the platform, saying, *"Sir I don't know you but I feel I'm here just to preach to you."* As he was preaching about the pro-life movement being the next movement from the civil rights movement, he begin to talk about God raising up African American prophets to trumpet this message like Dr. Martin Luther King Jr. in the 1960's.

That got my attention, because Dr. Martin Luther King Jr. had been a lifelong mentor of mine, who I had studied extensively for 15 years. Every tape, book, CD, Video, DVD that was out there, I had seen it, read it, and studied it. Dr. Martin Luther King had been the only person I had seen in modern, African-American Christendom that had really lived out the Sermon on the Mount lifestyle in the social order, and had given His life in the process for the cause of ending an unjust system in the earth. He was a preacher that I had seen boldly proclaim a message that he knew would eventually get himself or His family killed, yet he continued to speak and work towards the cause he believed God had given him. All the preachers that I knew were preaching a message that focused on escaping persecution and tribulation. I was raised in the theological foundation of bypassing hard times and persecution, and preached this message, even though I had inclinations and dreams against this thought pattern. I saw no one that exemplified an example of speaking out and taking a stand against an ungodly system regardless of what it cost them. Dr. King had served his generation with the message and life of Agape Love, the Love of God in the heart of men, and was slain for his life's work. Once this national speaker mentioned this great man of God and said "at the end of the age, many would go forth with the same spirit of boldness and fearlessness in the final generation, confronting false and counterfeit religious and political systems of the Harlot Babylon, I was all ears. Later that week I attended "this mass prayer gathering in a stadium in Cincinnati Ohio with my ministry team, at which time this man of God spotted me in the audience and called me up on the stage to help him pray for the coming together of African Americans and Caucasian ministers. After that event I sought to find out where the man of God was headquartered. Each time we talked we were unable to exchange correspondence. However, I was told that he was headquartered in Kansas City at a place called the International House of Prayer. This was a place I had been recently told by a visitor to our ministry that I should visit. They said because I emphasized prayer as the foundation of the things we did in the inner-city they thought I would really like this prayer ministry in Kansas City. Well, this speaker being from this ministry was a confirmation that I needed to visit this place called, "The International House of Prayer."

In April 2008 I visited I.H.O.P for the first time. When I got there, unbeknownst to me they were in the middle of the Israel Mandate conference. This was another confirmation, because of the calling I've felt to be a missionary to Israel since the early 1990's when I had the privilege to visit Israel. Immediately that got my attention. However, more than anything, what got my attention was the 24hr format of prayer and worship that I witnessed, lining up with the Wal-Mart analogy of the 21st century church. What I saw at IHOP lined up perfectly with the dream I had of worshippers and those gifted and talented in the arts coming into my father's little store front church lined up miles down the road to worship day and night. I was stunned with further confirmation when I found out that IHOP began in 1999 when God first had me close down my father's church for what

28

was coming in the 21st century. WOW! To say I was flabbergasted was a major understatement. I was totally captivated that weekend by everything.

In the midst of the Israel Mandate conference that weekend at IHOP God spoke to me through a speaker from Israel. He said I was going to be coming to Kansas City before I stepped out again to re-open my earthly Father's ministry, and that it would be a 24/7 house of prayer. But he said, *"Go home and wait upon God for the timing."* That was April 2008! It was over a year later, after a year of God walking me step by step off of a worldly system of provision and back to dependency on him, that I resigned in June of 2009. I resigned to begin preparation for this New Thing coming that God had shown me 9 years earlier, the pattern of the 21st century church being established in the earth upon the revelation of Jesus Christ, and as a House of Prayer for all nations.

To prepare for this mandate we moved to Kansas City Missouri on Nov. 20th 2009 to receive a time of training and preparation in establishing the 21st century prototype of the Tabernacle of David, a 24hr House of Prayer for all Nations. We submitted to this call to move to be a part of a unique prayer meeting, a modern day miracle, a ministry that has been in a prayer meeting for over 12 continuous years 24hrs a day, 7 days a week. The International House of Prayer is truly a sign and wonder in the earth, as men & women come from all the nations of the world to be a part of continuous worship, prayer and intercession. The primary mission at IHOP is: *To establish a 24/7 prayer room in Kansas City and throughout the nations of the world, as a solemn assembly that "keeps the fires on the altar burning til the return of the LORD" by gathering corporately to fast and pray in the spirit of the tabernacle of David, as God's primary method of establishing justice - full revival unto the Great Harvest (Amos 9:11-12; Acts 15:16)*

2008 truly was a prophetic year for me, a year of new beginnings, as God began revealing the structure of this new thing in the earth. There was also a prophetic sign in the earth to further encourage the church that this is a time to let go of old mindsets and ways of doing things. In our nation God shattered centuries of old paradigms in race relations with the electing of the first black President of the U.S. I believe this was a prophetic sign of the coming forth in the Church of our generation of the *New Thing* that will overtake the old. In the body of Christ many spoke of 2008 as *"The Year of New Beginnings"* and *"The Now Season for New Things*" was trumpeted throughout out the land by many, but in many cases we kept on doing the same ole things. Remember, In order to get verse 19, we must do verse 18 which says *"Remember not the former things, neither consider the things of old."*

In order to get the new thing we must *"BEHOLD IT"* (SEE IT). In order to behold it, or see it, we must *"remember not the former things"*, or let go of the old things, the old ways of doing it, old systems of operation, old paradigms of worship & ministry. For those who are willing to let go of the old, God will reveal and release the NEW! Unfortunately, most of the church has been continuing with church as usual, doing the same ole things. But for those who are spiritually perceptive they know something's not right with the church, something's changing, and something's shifting as our hearts cry out for the Real Jesus. As we pursue the New Wineskins for the new wine God will begin to reveal the 21st century structures that will position his body to return to His original intent in the earth – *A House of Prayer for all Nations built upon encountering the Glory of The Revelation of Jesus Christ.*

The End-Time Revival Prayer in the Spirit of the Tabernacle of David

In scripture whenever Israel went astray, God raised up spiritual reformers with a vision to restore worship as David commanded it, to enquire of the Lord in His temple, to behold the beauty of the Lord. All of the 7 "revivals" in Old Testament times restored Davidic worship towards this end. At the end of the age, God will release His end-time outpour of His Spirit that will bring the revival of the tabernacle of David in His House Prayer.

Amos (about 750 BC) prophesied of the restoration of David's Tabernacle and thus to reverse the damage of Israel's apostasy. The fullness of the Tabernacle of David speaks of Jesus' Millennial government over all nations that is based on 24/7 Davidic worship and intercession.

David's Revelation of Worship

As a young man, David made a vow to dedicate his life to find a resting place or dwelling place for God. This refers to a place where an unusual measure of God's presence is manifest on earth. David's life work was to establish a dwelling place for God in Jerusalem in his generation.

> *1 LORD, remember David and all his afflictions; 2 How he swore to the LORD, and vowed to the Mighty One: 3 "Surely I will not go into the chamber of my house, or go up to the comfort of my bed; 4 I will not give sleep to my eyes...5 until I find a place for the LORD, a dwelling place for the Mighty One of Jacob"...8 Arise, O, Lord, to Your resting place. (Ps. 132:1-8)*

31

David vowed to live in extravagant devotion to seek the Lord with all his resources (time, talents, treasures). His vow included spending time in God's House (Ps. 27:4), fasting (Ps. 69:7-12), extravagant giving of his money (1 Chr. 22:14) and embracing God's order in worship. This vow changed history and continues today in those who embrace it. It is at the heart of the End-Time worship movement. The Lord, will raise up a million believers who fully walk out this vow. David's vow positioned his heart to receive insight into the worship that God seeks.

> *23 True worshipers will worship the Father in spirit and truth; for the Father is seeking such to worship Him. (Jn. 4:23)*

David received revelation of worship in God's heavenly sanctuary (1 Chr. 28:11-19).

> *96 I have seen the consummation of all perfection (God's Throne of Glory)... (Ps. 119:96.) 11. David gave his son Solomon the plans...12 for all that he had by the Spirit, of the courts of the house of the LORD...13 also for the division of the priests and the Levites, for all the work of the service of the house of the LORD...19 All this," said David, "the LORD made me understand in writing, by His hand upon me, all the works of these plans." (1 Chr. 28:11-19)*

> *2 I heard a voice from heaven, like the voice of many waters, and...loud thunder. I heard the sound of harpists...3 They sang...a new song before the Throne... (Rev. 14:2-3)*

> *13 Every creature which is in heaven and on the earth...saying: "Blessing and honor...be toHim who sits on the Throne, and to the Lamb, forever and*

ever!" 14 The twenty-four elders fell down and worshiped Him who lives forever and ever. (Rev. 5:13-14)

The KJV says that God "inhabits (lives in or manifests His life) in the praise of His people. David taught that when we sing praise that God inhabits (manifests His power) in that context. *3. You are...enthroned (manifest the power of Your Throne) in the praises of Israel. (Ps. 22:3)*

David's revelation of heavenly worship (as seen in Psalms) is foundational to David's throne which is "political government in the spirit of the Tabernacle of David" or government based on 24/7 worship and intercession. David's government flowed forth from prophetic worship (1 Chr. 23-25). David had revelation of the spiritual impact of prophetic intercessory worship (Ps. 22:3).

6 Let the high praises of God be in their mouth... 7 to execute vengeance (justice) on the nations, and punishments on the peoples; 8 to bind their kings with chains...9 to execute on them the written judgment-- this honor have all His saints. (Ps. 149:6-9)

After David became king, the first thing he did was to capture Jerusalem (2 Sam. 5:3-10). Then he gave expression to his sacred vow by setting up a worship tabernacle in Jerusalem (2 Sam. 6). David received revelation from God about establishing God's order of worship first in Jerusalem. One of the first things that Jesus will do when He rules Jerusalem is to establish worship there.

1 David...prepared a place for the ark of God, and pitched a tent for it...16 David spoke to the...Levites to appoint...singers accompanied by instruments of music... (1 Chr. 15:1-16)

David put Levites before the Ark (which spoke of God's Throne and presence) to worship God.

> *1 They brought the ark...and set it in the midst of the tabernacle that David erected for it. 4 He appointed Levites (singers) to minister before the ark...to praise the Lord...37 to minister before the ark regularly, as every day's work required... (1 Chr. 16:1, 4, 37)*

David established 4,000 full-time paid musicians, 288 singers (12 x 24 = 288) and 4,000 gatekeepers.

> *7 The number...instructed in the songs of the Lord...who were skillful, was 288. (1 Chr. 25:7) 4,000 were gatekeepers, and 4,000 praised the Lord with musical instruments... (1 Chr. 23:5)*

David commanded God's people to honor the heavenly order of worship that he received by revelation because it was God's command (2 Chr. 29:25; 35:4, 15; Ezra 3:10; Neh. 12:45). These worship principles are timeless and valid today, such as establishing singers and musicians in God's House. The application of these principles would differ in each generation and culture.

> *25 Hezekiah...stationed Levites in the house of the Lord with stringed instruments... according to the commandment of David...for thus was the commandment of the Lord.(2 Chr. 29:25)*

David provided financial support so that singers could sing as a full-time occupation.

33 These are the singers...who lodged in the chambers, and were free from other duties; for they were employed in that work day and night. (1 Chr. 9:33)

God's order for supporting the singers and gatekeepers was revealed to David. The storehouse was the central place to receive tithes that was under the spiritual leadership of the Lord's House. Asaph and his brothers were included in the 288 singers (12 x 24 = 288).

37 So he left Asaph and his brothers there before the ark of the covenant of the LORD to minister before the ark regularly, as every day's work required... (1 Chr. 16:37)

Salvation into kingdom

David gave over $100 billion (according to today's prices) to God's House from his personal finances. One talent equals about 75 lbs or 1200 ounces (16 ounces in a pound). 100,000 talents weighed about 7.5 million pounds (almost 4,000 tons). At $700 an ounce, a talent of gold would be worth about $850,000. Thus, 100,000 talents of gold would be worth about $85 billion. A talent of silver at $12 an ounce is worth nearly $15,000, thus one million talents of silver (75 million pounds or almost 40,000 tons) is worth about $15 billion.

1 Indeed I have taken much trouble to prepare for the House of the LORD 100,000talents of gold ($85 billion) and 1,000,000 talents of silver ($15 billion)... (1 Chr. 22:14)

Financial Provision for the End Time Worship Movement

Once David received revelation of worship according to God's order in the heavenly sanctuary it was the key to release the wealth of Heaven on earth. Rev.4-5 describes the worship order around God's Throne. Those nearest God's Throne agree with Him in 24/7 worship and intercession as the most exalted occupation in the New Jerusalem. David gave his son Solomon these plans along with all the resources necessary for this endeavor.

> *for all that he had by the Spirit, of the courts of the house of the LORD...13 also for the division of the priests and the Levites, for all the work of the service of the house of the LORD... (1 Chr. 28:11-12)*

> *I have seen the consummation of all perfection (God's Throne of Glory)... (Ps. 119:96)*

The Cost of a Modern Day Tabernacle of David in Cities of Refuge

As David established 4,000 full-time paid musicians, 288 prophetic singers and 4,000 gatekeepers he was financing about 10,000 full-time staff to facilitate worship. Today it would cost about $200 million a year to provide $3,000 a month for 5,000 full-time people (plus buildings costs).

> *The number...instructed in the songs of the Lord...who were skillful, was 288. (1 Chr. 25:7) 4,000 were gatekeepers, and 4,000 praised the Lord with musical instruments... (1 Chr. 23:5)*

The storehouse was the central place to receive tithes under the leadership of the Lord's House.

> *The tithes...were commanded to be given to the Levites and singers and gatekeepers...10 I realized that the portions for the Levites had not been given them; for each of the Levites and the singers who did the work had gone back to his field. 11 So I contended with the rulers, and said, "Why is the house of God forsaken?" I gathered them together and set them in their place. 12 Then all Judah brought the tithe...to the storehouse... (Neh. 13:5-12)*

The Levites were commanded to tithe on what they received. They brought it to the storehouse. When we return to worship as it is in heaven, and begin to tithe so that worshippers can once again worship the Lord fulltime, 24/7 in His house before the Lord, there will be a great transfer of wealth in the End-Times as God shakes the nations, and releases the power to gain wealth to His people (Hag. 2:6-8).

> *The Levites receive tithes; and the Levites shall bring up a tenth of the tithes to the house of our God, to the rooms of the storehouse. (Neh. 10:38)*

> *I have given the children of Levi all the tithes...in return for the work which they perform, the work of the Tabernacle...26 Speak to the Levites, and say: 'When you take...the tithes...then offer...to the LORD, a tenth of the tithe..." (Num. 18:21-26)*

> *Return to Me, and I will return to you...You said, "In what way shall we return?" 8 Will a man rob God? Yet you robbed Me! You say, "In what way have we*

*robbed You?" In tithes and offerings. 9 You are
cursed with a curse, for you have robbed Me...10
Bring all the tithes into the storehouse, that there
may be food in My house, and try Me now in this...if
I will not open for you the windows of heaven and
pour out for you such blessing that there will not be
room enough to receive it. 11 I will rebuke the
devourer for your sakes... (Mal. 3:7-11)*

The Coming of Houses of Prayer at the End of the Age

Amos prophesied of the restoration of David's Tabernacle at the end of the age. Just as when Israel went astray, God raised up reformers who restored worship as David commanded, God, in the church at the end of age is going to raise up reformers who will restore worship once again as David commanded. All the 7 "OT revivals" restored this.

Solomon established the singers according to the direction that God gave his father David.

*According to the order of David his father, he
(Solomon) appointed...Levites for their duties to
praise...as the duty of each day required...for so
David...commanded. (2 Chr. 8:12-14)*

Josiah's revival (about 625 BC) restored full-time singers and musicians as David commanded. Jehoshaphat and Jehoiada restored worship in the order of David (2 Chr. 20:19-28; 23:16-18).

*He said to the Levites...4 "Prepare
yourselves...following the instruction of David..." 15
The singers...were in their places, according to the*

38

command of David... (2 Chr. 35:3-15) J. Zerubbabel established full-time singers and musicians as commanded by David (Ezra 3:10-11). Ezra and Nehemiah established full-time singers and musicians as David commanded.

The Levites...give thanks...according to the command of David...45 The singers and the gatekeepers kept the charge of God...according to the command of David... (Neh. 12:24, 45)

In the days of Zerubbabel and Nehemiah all Israel gave the portions for singers... (Neh. 12:47)

In May 1983, the Lord called IHOP-KC to establish the first 24/7 House of prayer in the spirit of the Tabernacle of David in the United States. In 1999 they actually launched out in this call. As a result many Houses of Prayer have begun popping up all over this nation and the world since that time as a prophetic sign at the end of the age of the preparation for the return of the Lord.

Embracing David's Revelation of Worship in the Old Testament

11 On that day I will raise up the Tabernacle of David, which has fallen down, and repair its damages; I will raise up its ruins, and rebuild it as in the days of old... (Amos 9:11)

Jesus requires night and day prayer as the condition to release justice. Prayer is a very practical expression of the commandment to love one another in that it releases deliverance for the needy. The revelation of intercession affected David's method of government. He established 24/7 worship and intercession as the foundation of his kingly reign in Israel (1 Chr. 23-25). His revelation of heavenly worship (as seen in Psalms) is foundational to David's throne which is "political government in the spirit of the Tabernacle of David" or government based on 24/7 prophetic worship and intercession. He had revelation of the power of worship (Ps. 22:3).

> *3 You are holy, enthroned (release power) in the praises (singing the Word) of Israel. (Ps. 22:3) 6 Let the high praises of God be in their mouth... 7 to execute vengeance (justice) on the nations, and punishments on the peoples; 8 to bind their kings with chains...9 to execute on them the written judgment-- this honor have all His saints. (Ps. 149:6-9)*

CHAPTER 3

CITIES OF REFUGE AND DELIVERANCE FROM THE SPIRIT OF THE WORLD – THE SPIRIT OF LEVIATHAN

Job 41:1 Canst thou draw out leviathan with an hook? or his tongue with a cord which thou lettest down? 2 Canst thou put an hook into his nose? or bore his jaw through with a thorn? 3 Will he make many supplications unto thee? will he speak soft words unto thee?

One night in October of 2012 I was awakened in the middle of the night with the urge to pray. Because it was so early I began to read in an attempt to stir my flesh to yield to my spirit that was obviously already stirred to pray. As I was reading in the book of Psalm, the spirit of prayer began to overtake my desire to sleep. As I began praying in the spirit, it appeared I fell back to sleep. But as I did, I instantly began to dream. In the dream I was on a City Bus, in my city of 1.6 million people. On the bus with me were parents of children I had been serving in a Consulting capacity through the Columbus Urban League, a non-profit Human services organization in my City. These parents were all telling me, *"Thank you for helping our city, for making a difference in our city."* As I was receiving their thanks and telling them *"You're Welcome,"* a lady bus driver looked at me with an evil stare and said, *"Yeah, Thanks for helping our City,"* *"Now, you better Hold on."* Then she took off. As she accelerated, she began driving the bus recklessly, narrowly missing pedestrians crossing the street. She was narrowly missing parked cars on the side of the street. She hit every bump in the road, tossing the passengers all over the bus. As I grabbed the handles on the side top bus

41

handle rails, I asked her why she was driving so recklessly, and pleaded with her to slow down. As she continued gaining speed, going faster and faster I could see we were heading towards a dead–end wall. As she saw the dead-end she slammed on the breaks and we began to come to a screeching halt. To miss a head-on collision with the wall, she turned the bus sideways narrowly missing slamming head-on into the wall. Once the bus came to a screeching halt, the wall became a movie screen. At that moment I woke up and the wall of that building was the wall at the head of my bed. On the wall/screen were the most hideous animals/creatures moving around in a swamp. As I looked closer, I tried to focus to see what kind of animals they were in the swamp. I had never seen anything living like the creatures I saw in that swamp. As I continued to try to focus to figure out what these creatures were, the vision on the wall began to slowly dissipate. I kept asking, *Wait! Wait! What is that? What is this I'm seeing*? Once the vision was gone, I kept asking the Spirit of the Lord all day, *"What was that?"* I heard the words in my Spirit say, *"This is the spirit holding back the Salvation of your City. This is the Spirit that is keeping your City from the true expression of what I've called for the purpose of this City and for every member of this City."*

I continued asking, "What is that Spirit? What is it, and what do you want me to do? I didn't hear anything that night. But several days later I was on Google looking up something on my computer for my Urban League responsibilities, when I saw a picture that looked strikingly similar to the vision on my bedroom wall. Under the picture it stated; "Destruction of Leviathan." by Gustave Dore. Immediately the Holy Spirit said, *"That's the spirit that's holding your city and the cities of the earth - The Spirit of Leviathan - from my expression and purpose for cities to be Holy Cities."* (On the next page is the picture similar to the one I saw that day, of Leviathan.)

42

The Spirit of Leviathan

As I began to study on the spirit of Leviathan, and what God meant by, "Holy Cities," I found out that Leviathan is mentioned 4 times in scripture; once in Job, twice in Psalms and once in Isaiah.

Depiction of Leviathan

"Destruction of Leviathan" by Gustave Dore'

Job 41:1 Canst thou draw out leviathan with an hook? or his tongue with a cord which thou lettest down? 2 Canst thou put an hook into his nose? or

43

bore his jaw through with a thorn? 3 Will he make many supplications unto thee? will he speak soft words unto thee?

4 Will he make a covenant with thee? wilt thou take him for a servant forever? 5 Wilt thou play with him as with a bird? or wilt thou bind him for thy maidens?

6 Shall the companions make a banquet of him? shall they part him among the merchants? 7 Canst thou fill his skin with barbed irons? or his head with fish spears? 8 Lay thine hand upon him, remember the battle, do no more.

9 Behold, the hope of him is in vain: shall not one be cast down even at the sight of him? 10 None is so fierce that dare stir him up: who then is able to stand before me?

11 Who hath prevented me, that I should repay him? whatsoever is under the whole heaven is mine. 12 I will not conceal his parts, nor his power, nor his comely proportion.

Job 41 calls Leviathan a sea monster, or beast in the sea, and says, who can pull the sea beast, Leviathan with a fly rod (MSG), and stuff him in your creel? Who can lasso him with a rope, or snag him with an anchor? God is speaking to Job about what Leviathan is, how he operates, and how He deals with him. Job reveals how Leviathan responds in flowery speech and flattery to resist his capture and defeat. Job says, Leviathan will apply for a job with His captors or those fighting against him. He will even run errands and serve them the rest of their lives; speaking of His entry way and operation into the earth, and the Church. God asks Job, "Will

44

you play with him as if he were a pet goldfish?" Will you make him the mascot of the neighborhood children? Will you put him on display in the market and have shoppers haggle over the price. This last phrase reveals that Leviathan is behind the economics in cities and nations. In the book of Job, God goes on to reveal how not to deal with Leviathan, and how to be delivered from the Spirit of Leviathan. Leviathan is also mentioned in Psalm 74:12 saying;

> *For God is my King of old, working salvation in the midst of the earth. 13 Thou didst divide the sea by thy strength: thou brakest the heads of the dragons in the waters. 14 Thou brakest the heads of leviathan in pieces, and gavest him to be meat to the people inhabiting the wilderness.*

God save Our Cities

Psalms 74 calls Leviathan the dragon in the waters and reveals how he is defeated. Psalm 74 connects the defeat of Leviathan with the salvation of the earth by God, saying, *"For God is my King of old, working salvation in the midst of the earth. You divide the sea by your Strength, and You break the head of the dragons in the waters, breaking the heads of leviathan in pieces."* Salvation of a people in a city, or in the earth, will not come until the Spirit of Leviathan is broken over cities. If the Spirit of Leviathan is not dealt with the people of that city will be held captive by this spirit. Even those that confess Jesus as Lord and attend Church. Cities and systems that operate in cities must be saved, as well as the people, in order for God's will to be accomplished in our regions, and our cities be protected in times of conflict. In scripture and in the mind of God, cities have personalities; Cities have a spirit, a soul, and a body. When God sent Jesus to save the people of the world His mission was not just the salvation of the people of the world, but of the world system, or the earth itself. When

Scripture calls Satan the god of this world, it's speaking of the system of the world. It's speaking of the orderly arrangement of this world. The earth is the Lord's, but He gave the earth as an inheritance to the children of men (Psa. 115:16). When Adam sinned, he did not just become separated from God because of sin, he also separated the earth God created from God, or from the Heavens. Adam gave the title deed or keys of authority in the earth to Satan. When God sent Jesus, he not only sent Jesus to redeem man from his sins, but also to redeem the earth back from Satan, to reconcile heaven and earth, and to give earths keys back to man.

Jerusalem – The Blueprint for Cities of Refuge

When Jesus came to the city of Jerusalem he wept over the city and spoke to the city, showing us that cities have a personality or a spirit;

> *O Jerusalem, Jerusalem, how I longed to come to you, to visit you, to gather you (to protect you) as a hen does her chicks, but you did not know the time of your visitation.* Luke 13:34

> *And when he was come near, he beheld the city, and wept over it, Saying, If thou hadst known, even thou, at least in this thy day, the things which belong unto thy peace! but now they are hid from thine eyes.* Luke 19:41, 42

It was the personality of religious pride and performance over Jerusalem from the religious systems operating in Jerusalem that caused that city to be unable to recognize that her salvation (Jesus) was in her midst. Jesus was actually crying out, interceding for the City of Jerusalem. He was not just crying out for the people of the city, but for the spirits that were binding the people

46

and purpose of that City, keeping her from recognizing the time of her visitation. When Jesus wants to visit a city with His presence, if the spirit over that city and the systems operating in that city are not dealt with, Jesus cannot have access into that City. When Jesus cried out over Jerusalem His intercessory cry, He was aware that in a few short years (70 A.D) Jerusalem would be ravaged, the temple would be destroyed and the blood sacrifices would cease. He knew that His people would not have a blood sacrifice, once the temple was destroyed, for over 2000 years, and their only covering would be His blood that He would soon shed on Calvary's cross. But because of their religious pride they could not recognize this transitional, generational shift that was taken place in their time. As a result there would be no refuge for what was coming to Jerusalem in 70 A.D. and over the next 2000 years. The whole city would be destroyed, and the nation would go through two millenniums of human atrocities where their own blood would be shed in the earth at the hands of evil, heinous, madmen set on their destruction.

The Peace of Jerusalem – A Refuge in the Time of War
Pray for the peace of Jerusalem...Ps. 122:6

The Hebrew word "Peace" in Psalm 122:6 does not mean the absence of war, but more appropriately, it means a refuge in the times of war. It means to be at one with, or atonement through the blood of Christ. It literally means to be reconciled to God through sacrificial bloodshed. The essence of this word *"peace"* is reconciliation of the whole through the sacrifice of one's blood or life. It is not the absence of war or conflict. Our westernized English interpretation of the word "peace" has often had many praying against conflict, war or bloodshed in Jerusalem. However, peace here actually has another connotation in the mind of God. It is the same connotation for peace given by the Holy Spirit through the Apostle Paul in Ephesians 2:13-15

> But now in Christ Jesus you who once were far
> away have been brought near by the blood of
> Christ.
>
> [14] **For he himself is our peace**, who has made the
> two groups one and has destroyed the barrier, the
> dividing wall of hostility, [15] by setting aside in his
> flesh the law with its commands and regulations.
> His purpose was to create in himself one new
> humanity out of the two, thus making peace, [16] and
> **in one body to reconcile both of them to God**
> **through the cross, by which he put to death their**
> **hostility.** Eph. 2:13-15

The word "peace" is speaking here of reconciliation of men to God
through the sacrifice of His Son. This peace being the
reconciliation of men to God and to one another is what destroys
the barrier or dividing wall of hostility between God and man. This
definition of peace is not often taken into consideration when
most believers pray for the peace of Jerusalem.

The Judgment coming before the Peace of Jerusalem

In Psalm 122:6 the command to pray for this peace or
reconciliation of Jerusalem to God is preceded by verse 5 which
says, there are set thrones or times of Judgment of the House of
David coming before peace. It's speaking of a set time of
Judgment that will come to Jerusalem, and its saying, during that
set time of Judgment coming to the house of David, pray that my
people will be reconciled to me. What is that Judgment? In the
Old Testament there were Judgments pronounced on the children
of Israel if they would leave the commands of God (Deut. 28:14-
56).

48

The way that Jesus gets access into cities is through the praying Churches of those cities. When Jesus cried out in Luke 19:41-46 because Jerusalem did not recognize her day of visitation, He then went to the Temple (the Church of that day), to visit the temple for the first time, as if to say, "Why isn't this City ready for my visitation?" When He got to the temple He found the religious leaders engaged in religious corruption, and he prepared a whipped and turned over the tables of the money changers and cried out. *"My House shall be called a House of Prayer, but you have made it a den of thieves."* (Luke 19:41-46)

Those that Love me in Jerusalem

The verse in Psalm 122:6 is actually speaking of a coming judgment on the people of God that will make even the Holocaust pale in comparison, but this time the resulting consequence will be more than a restoration to their homeland of the Jewish people, but a reconciliation of that land and God's people back to God himself, along with the return of their Messiah, Yeshua Hamashiach.

Psalm 122:5, 6 is actually addressing this Judgment when it directs prayers to be prayed for the peace of Jerusalem. The directive before and after the colon in Psalm 122:6 - ***Pray for the peace of Jerusalem: they shall prosper that love thee*** - is actually two prayer directives dealing firstly with how to pray during the coming Judgment, and secondly, who to pray for in Jerusalem during this time of Judgment – *those that love Him*. The first directive during the coming judgment is:

- Pray for the Peace of Jerusalem – Pray that the city in the time of Judgment is reconciled to God (peace).

- And the second directive after the colon is speaking of, prayer to be offered up for *those that already know Him and love Him (As Messiah and have received His blood as the judgment for their sins) in Jerusalem, that they will be kept secure from the Judgment.*

So, after the beginning of the set times of Judgment from verse 5, (*there are set thrones of Judgment, the thrones of the House of David-Psalm 122:5*) Pray for the Peace (reconciliation) of Jerusalem to God, and pray that those that love me and already have been reconciled to me in Jerusalem are kept secure.

A House of Prayer for All Cities

From the prayer we are commanded to pray in Psalm 122:6 we can see how God expects all cities to become cities of refuge in times of conflict in the earth, by praying for and comforting Jerusalem in her time of conflict and trouble. From Jesus' first coming to the earth we can see how God expects the House of Prayer to prepare cities for His return. We can see how cities must be prepared for their visitation and salvation from the Lord, just as individual people must invite Jesus to come into their hearts and lives. This is done over cities by dealing with the Spirit that holds cities captive from recognizing Jesus as their blood covering – *The Spirit of Leviathan.* Psalm 74 says, God is My King from long ago, working salvation on the earth, breaking the heads of the monster of the waters, crushing the heads of Leviathan. This verse gives us the key for dealing with this spirit over cities. "GOD IS MY KING." We must see Jesus as the King of kings, and Lord of lords. He must be King in the hearts of His people. He must be King of those that He's looking to pray and intercede for the breaking of the spirit that holds the people of a city from recognizing His visitation. Without a people that have made God King, God has no access into our Cities. The Spirit of Leviathan is defeated by making God your King, or ruler of every part of your life, allowing him to work salvation in the midst of the earth;

speaking of the people in the earth, as well as the systems in the earth through our obedience to Him as Lord and King of our lives.

Obedience and the Lordship of Jesus

> *But why do you call Me "**Lord, Lord**," and **do not do** the things which I say?* . . . *Go therefore and make disciples of all the nations, baptizing them* . . . *[and] **teaching** them to **observe all things** that I have commanded you; and lo, **I am with you always**, even to the end of the age.* (<u>Luk 6:46</u> *and* <u>Mat 28:19-20</u>)

As servants of the new covenant of grace, the Lordship of Jesus is part of our message. "For we do not preach ourselves, but Christ Jesus **the Lord**" (<u>2Co 4:5</u>). The early church proclaimed Jesus as **Lord**. "Therefore let all the house of Israel know assuredly that God has made this Jesus, whom you crucified, both **Lord** and Christ . . . The word which God sent to the children of Israel, preaching peace through Jesus Christ — He is **Lord** of all . . . believe on the **Lord** Jesus Christ, and you will be saved . . . Then Paul dwelt two whole years . . . teaching the things which concern the **Lord** Jesus Christ" (<u>Act 2:36</u>; <u>Act 10:36</u>; <u>Act 16:31</u>; and <u>Act 28:30-31</u>).

The scriptures often emphasize the fact that Jesus is our **Lord**. The opening verses of Paul's first letter to Corinth are a clear example. "*Paul* . . . *to those who are sanctified in Christ Jesus* . . . *with all who in every place call on the name of Jesus Christ **our Lord*** . . . *Grace to you and peace from God our Father and **the Lord** Jesus Christ* . . . *you come short in no gift, eagerly waiting for the revelation of **our Lord** Jesus Christ* . . . *who will also confirm you to the end, that you may be blameless in the day of **our Lord** Jesus*

51

*Christ. God is faithful, by whom you were called into the fellowship of His Son, Jesus Christ **our Lord**. Now I plead with you, brethren, by the name of **our Lord** Jesus Christ" (1Co 1:1-10).*

Clearly, it is right for followers of Jesus to call Him Lord. Yet, to call Him Lord and then disobey Him is a contradiction. "But why do you call Me '**Lord, Lord**,' and do not do the things which I say?" After believing in Jesus and identifying with Him in water baptism, disciples are to be growing in obedience: "teaching them to observe all things that I have commanded you." As we are learning to walk in obedience, Jesus is ever present with us. "I am with you always." Day by day, He offers the grace we need for obedience: "Declared to be the Son of God with power . . . through whom we have received grace and apostleship for obedience to the faith" (Rom 1:4-5).

> *Lord Jesus, I long for my verbal confession of Your Lordship to be validated by my daily growth in obedience. You are my Master. Grant me grace each day to be obedient to the faith, in Your sovereign name I pray, Amen.*

Psalms reveals that as a result of Leviathans rule the people in those cities and regions inhabit the wilderness. But it goes on to reveal the provision that will come to those inhabitants in the wilderness by Leviathan's defeat.

The Defeat of Leviathan will come before Jerusalem Becomes a Praise in the Earth
Isaiah 27-29

> *In that day the Lord with His severe sword, great and strong, will punish Leviathan, the fleeing*

serpent, Leviathan that twisted serpent; And He will slay the reptile that is in the sea

In that day sing to her, a vineyard of red wine! I, the Lord, will keep it, I water it every moment; lest any hurt it, I keep it night and day....Those who come He shall cause to take root in Jacob; Israel shall blossom and bud, and fill the face of the world with fruit.

In Isaiah 27-29 the Prophet connects the restoration of the nation of Israel, as well as all the cities of the earth to the slaying of this spirit of Leviathan. Over the next several pages I want to submit a sermon by Steve Bell, which I believe describes what this spirit of Leviathan actually is and How he is to be dealt with in the minds and hearts of God's people that have made Him King of their lives.

Leviathan Represents or Burrows into the Self of Man.

In the book of Job the whole context is an ongoing debate between Job and his friends. Finally, God announces that He has had enough and demands an answer in chapter 38:4: "Where was thou when I laid the foundations of this earth? Declare if thou has understanding." In verse 31 He asks, "Canst thou bind the sweet influences of Pleiades or loose the bands of Orion?"**Here at the culmination of an entire revelation, God gives this righteous man of God an entire discourse about leviathan.** Some call him a crocodile or something else, but he is an evil spirit. There is revelation here and although we do not have all of it, we can utilize what we do know.

Pride and the Spirit of Leviathan

When we get down to the real, true self, we are where leviathan has his stronghold. He's a writhing serpent, seven heads, etc. There is a part deep inside where leviathan dwells.

Even after ousting him, there's still self-will which says, "This as far as I'm willing to go," and sure enough, if you listen; that is as far as you will go. Job 41:8 says that when we lay our hands on leviathan we will remember the battle and will not do it again. That struggle reminds us of our old self who does not want to reveal things, does not want anyone to know.

Job 41:15 states that the scales of leviathan are his pride and are shut up together with a close seal. One is so near to another that no air can come between them.

In the scripture, air, breath and wind are synonymous with the Holy Spirit. The reason people get so shut in is because of the effects of leviathan's tight coils around them, inhibiting the moving of the Spirit. They cannot hear or discern the Spirit and they say they never get a word from the Lord or move in the gifts. The reason is that no air of the Spirit is able to get in because this demon has such a strangle hold.

The scales are joined one to another and cannot be sundered. "He makes a path to shine after him and one would think the deep to be hoary (or have white hair; to have wisdom with old age); upon earth there is not his like, who is made without fear, or (who behave without fear). He beholds all high things: he is a king over all the children of pride (vs. 32-34).

Another way of stating this is that he looks down on all who are haughty; he is a king over all those who are proud. Pride and leviathan are practically synonymous. It is hard to separate them because pride causes that stony heart to close the scales and folds

54

together blocking the Spirit of God from entering. Some sit listening, but not understanding or hearing the Word of God. Leviathan's most crucial work is in the area of keeping people from receiving the things of God and of the Spirit because of Pride. It's foolishness to them.

Attitudes Connected to the Leviathan Spirit

1. *Condescending attitudes toward others in the body.*
2. *Independent attitude.*
3. *Self -Glory*
4. *Self-Confidence*
5. *Lack of time in His presence*
6. *Critical and condemning attitudes and thoughts*
7. *Boasting over achievements and revelation*
8. *Dishonor of authority*
9. *Desiring to be served*
10. *Desire for reputation*
11. *Desiring to control others*
12. *Use of position of authority or gift to fulfill selfish Ambition and vision*
13. *Mocking or coming against Deliverance and/or Deliverance ministries*

The Spirit that Keeps God's People from coming together in Cities

Leviathan / pride

This is, in essence, the attitudes and the spirit that Jesus saw in the Temple when He came to the Temple of Jerusalem after He saw that the city was not ready for His appearing in the first century. The religious leaders of that day had condescending attitudes towards the common people. There was an independent attitude in the religious leaders, a desire for self-glory. They were critical and condemning in their attitudes and thoughts, boasting over their achievements and revelation. They had a desire for reputation and were using their position of authority or gifts to fulfill selfish ambition and vision. As a result, the City and the spirit of the City were not ready to receive their visitation.

As we look at the state of most of the body of Christ in the nations of the earth, this is still the state of most churches and leaders in the body of Christ of most cities in the 21st century. Our Churches in our cities have not become a House of Prayer for all Nations, preparing our cities for Jesus' visitation, because we are filled with the same spirit of religious pride that the religious leaders in the first century had. We can't come together as the body of Christ in most cities because of this Spirit of Pride that is operating in the church today.

It is a spirit of performance, a spirit of boasting over achievements and revelation, a desire for reputation, a desire to control others, to use positions and gifts to fulfill selfish ambition and vision. This is the spirit that is keeping the body of Christ in most cities divided and ineffective in preparing our cities for God's salvation to come to our cities. In order for God's salvation to come to our cities, the Churches of our cities must be delivered from the spirit of Leviathan, and come together, free from Pride, Self-Glory, Self-Confidence, attitudes of Independence and a desire to control, to work together as a city Church to make God's House a House of prayer, preparing our cities for His visitation. The counteracting spirit and attitude that must be prevalent in order for the Leaders of the religious community to come together to prepare their cities for God's visitation are listed on the next page.

COUNTERATTACK: by living in humility. James 4:10
Humble yourselves in the sight of the Lord and he will lift
you up.

- *Humble yourself daily*
- *Be accountable to others*
- *Be subject to wise counsel from mature leadership*
- *Continue in prayer daily asking God to reveal your*
  heart to you for assessment and correction.
- *Study and line up your life with the Word of God.*

When we get free from the Spirit of Leviathan we will see an outpour of the Spirit of God, and a release of the spirit of Love, Unity and the commanded blessing on a people, city or region.

How to be delivered from the Spirit of Leviathan

The book of Job gives us the keys for being delivered from the Spirit of Leviathan, which I believe are also the keys for preparing cities to endure the coming systemic collapse, building cities of refuge in the nations of the earth. The book of Job, detailing the plight of Job is actually the story of His deliverance from the Spirit of Leviathan. Leviathan is mentioned in Job more than any book. In Job 3 reference is made to leviathan as a dragon. In Job 38-41 Leviathan is mentioned more than any other passages in scripture. Why is this? Because Job's story is actually a story of the process God takes Job through to set him free from the Spirit of Leviathan.

Leviathan – The Spirit of Pride

Remember, the Spirit of Leviathan is the spirit in the world, which is the Spirit of Pride, or as 1 John 2:16 states, the lust of the flesh, lust of the eyes, and Pride of life. This spirit of Pride is the spirit that is in the world as a result of Satan becoming the God of this world, once he deceived Eve and Adam. This is the Spirit that causes us to be prideful or haughty in our achievements, or as a result of what we've attained, or the things we've accrued. The process that God took Job through towards his deliverance from the Spirit of Leviathan was not a process that was distinctive to Job. Neither was it necessarily because Job's actions were sinful. Job did not sin in word or deed but God knew that Job still needed to be delivered from the Spirit that was in the world. God offered up Job to go through this process because Job desired to live for God with all of his heart. Job actually qualified to go through this process. He was testified of to Satan by God himself, that *"He was a man that feared God, eschewed evil, and walked uprightly."*

However, Job was in the world, and Satan is the God of this world. Satan's job description is to steal, kill and destroy. In Job 2 Satan approached the throne with the sons of God (angels), and God asked Him what he was doing? Satan stated that he had been going to and fro throughout the earth......seeking whom he may devour. However, God's process into the Kingdom of God from the kingdom of darkness is actually the process of the wilderness, where we experience the death of the loss of Life as we know it. We experience the loss of fame, fortune, name, or reputation that brings a Humility that's able to be resurrected by God's grace, to a place where we're able to handle the eternal power, position and prosperity of the Kingdom of God, with a grace and humility that keeps us looking to serve God and man with our power.

However, Job was in the world and all he had attained and accrued, he had attained in the world, attached to the Spirit of the World. And concerning the spirit of the world, 1st John tells us that the Spirit of this world is a three-fold trinity, similar to, but not comparable to, the trinity represented in the Godhead. The trinity of Evil represented in the Spirit of this World is, ***the Lust of the Flesh, the Lust of the Eyes, and the Pride of Life***. Leviathan is simply the spiritual force behind this threefold manifestation of Evil, which is the Pride of Life in the earth, the personification of Satan's tactics manifesting to destroy mankind. Leviathan keeps man from His purpose in submitting to and serving God, submitting to and using the gifts of God for God's purposes and glory, and he keeps man from the purposes of humanity submitting to and serving one another. The spirit of Leviathan keeps us from submitting to no one but ourselves, using our gifts for our own selfish purposes, and subverting, controlling and dominating over one another to keep each other down and separated from God and one another. This, in a nutshell, is the purpose and M.O. of the spirit of Leviathan.

Everyone connected to, and born into this world, comes subject to and influenced by this spirit of Leviathan. The only way to get free from this spirit is to be born again, and get processed into the Kingdom of God from the Kingdom of darkness, comparable to the Children of Israel coming out of Egypt and going through the wilderness to their promised-land. They were being processed to be freed from that Spirit of Leviathan obtained while under the oppression and domination of the Egyptian system.

Job's life is the story of him being processed by God, from the Spirit of the world, and of Leviathan, to the Spirit of God and of His Kingdom. Job's life seemed perfect and intact. His life seemed spiritual and disciplined. However, Job, though He was an upright man that eschewed evil and walked uprightly, his life was still short of the kingdom.

The Process of Deliverance from the Spirit of Leviathan

As was stated above, the process of deliverance from the Spirit of Leviathan is the process of the wilderness, where we experience the death of the loss of name, fame, fortune and reputation. This is what Jesus voluntarily submitted to and experienced when He came into the earth as a man. Philippians 2:6 shows us His process in coming to the earth:

> *Who, being in very nature God, did not consider equality with God something to be used to his own advantage; rather, he made himself nothing by taking the very nature of a servant, being made in human likeness. And being found in appearance as a man, he humbled himself by becoming obedient to death- even death on the cross. Therefore God exalted him to the highest place and gave him the name that is above every name, that at the name of Jesus every knee should bow, in heaven and on earth and under the earth, and every tongue acknowledge that Jesus Christ is Lord, to the glory of God the Father.*

This process that Jesus submitted to was the process necessary to have power to overcome the spirit of the world. This process is what Jesus modeled throughout His life and ministry, from 12 years old, in Luke 2, when he went down from the temple and was subject to Mary and Joseph, to 30 years old when He submitted to the Spirit's leading to the wilderness for 40 days and 40 nights, on to the garden of Gethsemane and the Cross, when he submitted to the father's will that he would go to the cross as the lamb slain before the foundation of the world. Jesus submitted to the process necessary to overcome, be delivered from and eventually defeat the Spirit of Leviathan in the earth, which would enable Him to go through the Cross and defeat Satan Himself.

This is the same process that Jesus submitted to the rich young ruler when he answered Him wisely, after Jesus had answered his question, "What must I do to inherit eternal life?" Jesus stated, first, "keep the commandments." The young ruler said, "Teacher, all these I have kept since I was a boy." Jesus looked at him and loved him, and said, "One thing you lack," Go, sell everything you have (loss) and give to the poor, and you will have treasure in heaven. Then come and follow me. At this the man's face fell. He went away sad, because he had great wealth. His great wealth was attached to the Spirit of the world, the spirit of Pride that he identified as his status, position and fame in society. This spirit of Leviathan, or spirit of Pride, would keep him from following Jesus completely. He followed the teachings of the Law from his youth, but was unable to follow Jesus – *the Law from His heart* - when it called for him being asked to give up his status, his fame, his fortune and his reputation. This was the process Jesus was offering and presenting to the rich young ruler to get into the kingdom of God, where his life would have been resurrected, to be given a hundredfold, everything he would have loss or left, when he gave it all to the poor (Luke 10:30). However, to get to that place it would have required him being processed through the death of loss. This is what Jesus was referring to when He spoke to the crowd that it was easier for a rich man to go through the eye of a needle than to enter into the kingdom of heaven. The understanding of what Jesus was saying in this verse goes beyond the surface, and beyond our westernized understanding.

The Eye of the Needle and the Spirit of Leviathan

In the Middle East during Jesus' day, the eye of the needle was not a needle that was used to sew clothes. In the Middle East, in Jesus' day, the eye of the needle was a gate that was about five feet high that camels would have to stoop down and strip down to enter a city. The eye of the needle was at the entrance of a city. When a man would come into a city with his possessions loaded down on his camel, the possessions would have to be taken off of the camel, the camel would have to stoop down to go through the eye of the needle, and the possessions that were on the camel had to be carried through the gate one by one by hand.

Jesus was saying that the rich who come to God have to humble themselves and take off those things they have been carrying, to which many times they have been hiding behind. Those riches are often times coverings to cover up the inner poverty of their spirit. When we come into the kingdom of God we must humble ourselves and strip down. Because of the spirit of the world, those that come into the kingdom with riches, which they have gotten corruptly, even if they've done business honestly from the world's standards. It's still attached to the spirit in the world that says, "*We must produce and sell more to get more.* " While the system of the kingdom of God says, "*Give and it shall be given unto you (Luke 6:38)* – "*We must produce and Give more to get more.*"

For those individuals that come into the kingdom with more stuff attained through the operation of the spirit of the world, when they begin to walk in righteousness and do things God's way, they often-times have to lose and go down in their material and financial position. However, when they begin to understand what God's ways are and start doing things God's way, they soon are raised up by the Spirit of God as a witness that God's way leads to a greater level of wealth and abundance than they even had before they came to God, but it's detached from the Spirit of the world, and it's characterized by the spirit of giving in abundance, giving more than they keep or own. This is the process of deliverance from the spirit of Leviathan – *the death of loss.* This is what God knew Job was ready and able to endure, because God saw Job's heart, that he was a man that feared God, eschewed evil and walked uprightly. Therefore, God suggested to Satan Job's life as a life that was ready to be processed, to be delivered from the Spirit of the world, or Leviathan.

CHAPTER 4

THE SPIRIT OF LEVIATHAN AND BREAKING DOWN RELIGIOUS AND RACIAL DIVISIONS IN THE CITY CHURCH

Leviathan beholds all high things: he is a king over all the children of Pride - Job 40:32-34

One of the greatest manifestations of the Spirit of the World and of Leviathan in the earth is religious and racial pride that produces religious and racial divisions, separation, denominations and discrimination in the earth, and in the Church of Jesus Christ. When we get free from the Spirit of Leviathan we will see an outpour of the Spirit of God, which will release the spirit of Love, unity and the commanded blessing over people, cities and whole regions in the earth.

The Spirit of Leviathan in Religious and Racial Pride

In November 2011 at a 24hr Prayer meeting of 40,000 people in Detroit Michigan, during one of the twelve 2 hour prayer sessions, there was a time of prayer for the reconciliation of the blacks and whites in our nation. It was a very intense time, as a noted African-American Bishop in Detroit recounted the history of racism in America, with Slavery, share-cropping and Jim Crow laws, and in Detroit, with industrial share cropping with the Ford Motor Company and Henry Ford. At the end of this time of retrospection of America's unfortunate history of racism and discrimination this African-American Bishop turned to the white ministers on the platform and said, "My father, who is 96 years old, told me to forgive white people for what they did to our forefathers, and if I would forgive without anyone apologizing, he said one day a white person would apologize to me for what

63

white people have done to our forefathers. " He then turned to the white ministers on the platform and said, "So now I want you to apologize to me." At that time many of the white ministers began to graciously oblige his request by apologizing and asking for forgiveness on behalf of what their forefathers did to our forefathers. After this, a young African-American minister on the platform felt the need to also apologize to the white ministers on the platform for what African-Americans have held against white people for what they had done to our forefathers. He referred to it as "REVERSE RACISM," saying he struggled with marrying his wife, who happened to be of European-descent, because of how he felt his family and friends would think of him marrying a white woman. He stated that many African-Americans struggled with these feelings about marrying outside of their race because of how they will be perceived, both by African-American women, and by bitter, unforgiving African-Americans in general.

He also went on to state that many African-Americans that voted for President Barak Obama just because he was Black operated in the same spirit of White prejudice and racism that has been perpetuated upon African-Americans for years. When he asked if all the African-American ministers could come together for a time of reconciliation, to apologize to our white brethren and pray for this counter thought pattern of prejudice, bitterness and reverse racism to be broken over our people, he was resisted by an older African-American Bishop, also from the city of Detroit. This Bishop stated that African-Americans should not have to apologize for any counter feelings of prejudice, bitterness or so-called "Reverse Racism," because we are the ones that have been unjustly treated, and we've never received a formal apology. And no, doubt, he said, her family probably didn't want her to marry you, as much as your family had reservations about you marrying her.
To say the least, this was a very intense time between these two people groups represented, being played out before 40,000

people on the stage at Ford Field in Detroit, and before millions by way of satellite T.V. and the live web-stream.

Racisms Religious Roots

At this time, and in this setting, I was asked to share my testimony of deliverance from these same feelings of prejudice, bitterness and un-forgiveness, which took place 20 years prior in my life. This chapter is the basis for what I shared at this Prayer gathering in Detroit, Michigan about what I believe is the roots of racism, as well as what I believe is the spirit behind racism that must be overcome for cities to come together to establish Cities of Refuge and Goshen communities in the day of a coming systemic collapse. I began sharing by stating that racism did not begin with Slavery, the Share-cropping system, or Jim Crow laws.

Jesus Stands Against Racism

One of the earliest examples of racism in modern History (A.D.) actually began with religion. And one of the strongest statements for racial reconciliation was actually spoken by Jesus Christ Himself dealing with religious exploitation in God's house of prayer in the New Testament, Mark 11:17. Jesus Christ uttered one the most profound statements about the inclusion of all racial groups in his house of prayer, quoting from Isaiah 56:7, when He said, *"My house shall be called of ALL NATIONS the house prayer."* The word, *"All Nations"* is the Greek word *"Ethnos,"* which is where we get our English word, "Ethnic or Ethnicity," meaning people or racial groups. I don't believe Jesus only made this statement because of the corruption of the merchandising of animal sacrifices alone, which was going on in the temple during that time. Jesus was not only upset because of this buying and selling that was taking place in the temple, but I believe he was also just as upset because of where in the temple it was taking place. They were using the courts of the Gentiles to buy and sell animal sacrifices for the Holy days. The courts of the Gentiles were where the Gentiles were allowed to come and pray. This area was now being used by the Jewish religious leaders for unjust monetary gain for the temple, exploiting the Gentiles, while keeping them from coming to the House of God, probably out of their disdain and racists attitudes for the Gentiles. In this religious community and place of worship, racists' attitudes were actually interfering with the Gentiles coming to the house of prayer. The premier verse displaying Jesus' righteous indignation in scripture was displayed against racism in the house of God. We often quote the first part of this statement, *"My house shall be called a house of prayer,"* but forget or overlook the latter part of that verse which says, *"FOR ALL NATIONS."* This part of Jesus' statement reveals the purpose of God's house, as well as God's chosen nation, Israel – *to be a light to the Nations (Gentiles).* This phrase; *"For all Nations"* is as important as the first part of this statement made by Jesus, because it reveals what was actually the focus of His displeasure. The Gentile nations were being discriminated against and inhibited from coming to God's house, keeping God's house from the power of its purpose – *PRAYER FOR ALL NATIONS TO BE RECONCILED TO GOD.* Thusly God's house was not fulfilling its purpose as a House of Prayer *FOR ALL NATIONS.*

Defining Racism

Racism is one of the most subtle and misunderstood enemies that operates under the control of this Spirit of Leviathan to keep people groups and churches divided and against one another. If we're going to get free in our generation, or in any generation from this expression of the spirit of Leviathan – Racism – we're going to have to uncover and understand racism and how it functions and operates, both in the world and in the church, to keep people groups divided and at odds with one another. What really is Racism? Most people that define or think of racism and label people as racists are actually not thinking about racism, but

Prejudice or Bigotry. I believe the definition that best defines racism was given by the educator Paul Kivel in his book *"Uprooting Racism:"* **Racism** *is the institutionalization of social injustice based on skin color, other physical characteristics, or cultural and religious differences.*

Dr. Claud Anderson, a black educator and economic development consultant, said something along similar lines in his book, *"Black Labor, White Wealth,"* saying; **Racism** *is a power relationship or struggle between groups of people who are competing for resources and political power. It's one group's use of wealth, power and resources to deprive, hurt, injure, and exploit another group to benefit itself.*

An Unrealized Dream

It is this operation of the spirit of Leviathan – Racism – that must be overcome at the end of the age, in key cities of Refuge in the earth, to prepare cities to come together in unity within the body of Christ, to endure the coming systemic collapse. In the 1960's civil rights movement, in the midst of the struggle for desegregation in American society, Dr. Martin Luther King Jr. famously declared that "11 o'clock on Sunday morning is the most segregated hour of the week." Sadly, this still holds true, even today, 50 years after the desegregation of public facilities in America. In the church which has lost its purpose and has cultivated a culture of prayerlessness, we still have a racially segregated Church in America, keeping the church from her purpose as a place of prayer for all nations. What's even sadder for African-American Christians and unbelievers alike is that though the walls of segregation were removed by the sacrifice of our forefathers in the civil rights movement, who gave their lives to assure that we would have some of the civil liberties and privileges we have today, the church in this generation still gravitates to our segregated houses of worship. Our forefathers sacrificed being ridiculed, terrorized, homes and churches bombed, beaten, and some even killed, so that the walls of partition and separation keeping racial groups divided would be torn down in this nation, and so that we could be integrated into American society. Yet, in many circles of society today African-Americans still acclimate to our segregated public accommodations.

No place is this acclimation to segregation in the public square seen more than in our segregated Churches. Our Churches are still the most segregated hour of the week. Our Church leaders still operate and run our churches by a bankrupt religious system that keeps our churches doctrinally and racially segregated, and many of our attendees and members still prefer these segregated churches. Though some of this is due to some systemic and economic demographics still at work in our society that keeps our neighborhoods segregated, by in large, we are still segregated in our churches because of either, the fear of stepping out of our racial comfort zones, religious tradition and control, or cultural worship preferences that we are unwilling to let go of. And in some cases we're still segregated within our churches because our church leaders still struggle with bitterness, and un-forgiveness that they are unwilling to let go of to assure that integration within the body of Christ is the norm in the church, and not the exception.

Coming Out Of My Racial Comfort Zone

Having grown up in the church I know firsthand how you can be a Christian whose faith has at the center of its worship a Jewish man who is of another ethnicity (Jewish) from 97% of his followers, (Gentiles) and still struggle with racial and religious bigotry and prejudice towards other racial groups. I know how as a Christian you can still be struggling with bitter feelings of un-forgiveness against other races for what was done to my ancestors, while claiming to worship a man who died on the cross for our sins, saying, "Father forgive them, for they know not what they do." This was my experience growing up in my African-American Church expression of Christianity.

As an African-American my experience with bitterness and un-forgiveness against Caucasians was not as a result of any personal negative experiences with racial discrimination, or prejudice. My bitterness and un-forgiveness against Caucasians was actually cultivated within my religious, African-American church experience. My sour racial mindsets stemmed from the fact that within our church upbringing there was a culture of distain and bitterness towards what was done to my ancestors, which was a part of our church culture. We were always talking about what Caucasians were doing to hold us back, or what they had done to us in the past. Consequently, in our church setting we had no desire to associate or interact with other races, even though in society the races had been desegregated for over 40 years. Growing up in the 1980's I really cannot identify one single personal experience with racism that I could point to and say, "They're trying to hold me back." Again, that's not to say that the system wasn't stacked against me. However, there were no personal experiences that would cause me to harbor bitter or unforgiving thought patterns towards Caucasians. And even though many in my family down through the years had experienced atrocious and tragic experiences at the hands of racially discriminative acts of persecution in Slavery, Jim Crow era, and Civil rights, I seemed to be aware that their experiences had paved the way for my generation, to continue the fight for a new era of justice and liberty for all. However, in our churches and communities we were still segregated, and we wanted to keep it that way. With our church leaders not wanting us to go outside of our comfort zone to foster relationships with people of other ethnicities, I built my racial worldview exclusively on my association with preachers and teachers in our church denomination and culture who were still bitter, offended and distrustful from their experiences, or their parents and grandparents experiences with Caucasian people. So I grew up dealing with these bitter, distrustful and prejudicial thought patterns towards Caucasians because I had never been outside of my racial culture to experience any positive inner-racial relationships. While I didn't have any negative experiences with discrimination, I did not have any positive experiences either, that would empower me to see Caucasian people the way God saw them. Our church bred in us an "us against them" mentality, in how we lived, how we worshipped, preached, prayed, and how we voted politically.

This Is Where I'm Sending You

This all began to change when my father started his own church in 1987 when I was 21 years old. I remember the first time I was challenged to come out of my familiar cultural surroundings. I was in my second year of ministry and desiring to go to Bible College. I had been praying about where God wanted me to go. One day I went to the mail box to get the mail at my parents' house and retrieved a magazine sent to my baby sister, who was 12 years old. The magazine was from a ministry on the outskirts of town that I had never heard of. On the front of the magazine it had the pastor in a preaching pose, and 7 characteristics of the church of the 90's. It was 1990 and the magazine intrigued me because I had just finished a message on the church of the 1990s and the coming glory of this decade. Everything that God had given me to preach was in the magazine article. On the back it had 10 reasons why you should come to this church's Bible institute. I heard the spirit of God speak up in my spirit and say, "THIS IS WHERE I'M SENDING YOU TO BIBLE COLLEGE." Immediately I began to make excuses for why I could not go to this Bible College. It was not an accredited institution and I was almost finished with College courses at an accredited State College in my City. Our church did

70

not believe the same way concerning baptism, which was a major stronghold in the denomination I had grown up in. We were Oneness Apostolic. We worshipped one way and they worshipped another way. Our church was small and theirs a mega church. But what I was afraid of most of all was that our church was African-American and theirs was Caucasian-Anglo-Saxon, and I had never been outside of my race for any type of church or religious experience.

Obeying the Leading of the Lord

I thought that I had a way out of going to this school. My father was my pastor and I thought that he would never let me go to that church bible Institute because of the differing beliefs. Doctrinally, we were staunchly against Trinitarians, (which we thought was the teaching of the belief in three gods), and against anyone that didn't baptize in Jesus name. We didn't fellowship with anyone who didn't believe the same as us in these areas. So when I went to my father and told him what God was speaking to me, I thought he would say, "We don't believe the same, so I would advise against it." Instead he said, "If God is dealing with you about going to school out there, you need to obey the leading of the Lord." Well, to say the least I was very nervous about this step out of my comfort zone, but I obeyed the Lord and enrolled in this Bible College. I was one of about 10 African-Americans in the student body of about 500 students. However, through the spirit of God I began to feel increasingly comfortable in this new setting and surrounding I was placed in. I began to develop friendships with those of other races, denominations, and cultures. I soon realized that I was missing a proper understanding of other cultures, teachings and ethnic expressions of worship. My heart began to be knitted to the Lord's heart concerning other nations, races and other aspects of Christ's nature. I began to know the Lord in a way I had never known him before. My relationship with the Lord increased what seemed like 10-fold. I began receiving revelation

71

from the Lord concerning His mission and calling for the nations of the world. I began to desire to pray and seek His face as I never had before. As a result of seeking the Lord in this manner, I began to realize that every ethnicity, people group, and denomination is a unique part of Christ. I understood that we won't see the body of Christ functioning fully, until we come together in unity. I also learned that each ethnicity, denomination, and culture is a piece of the puzzle and a key that unlocks our own individual and corporate destinies in Christ. We were created to need one another to fulfill what God has called us to do and to be.

I was delivered from fear, bitterness, and prejudice, just by being in the midst of another ethnic expression and developing heart relationships with people outside of my own ethnicity. I learned what the Love of God is and what it is for, as I saw John 3:16 through the lens of the whole world, not just my little part of the world. John 3:16 says, "God, so Loved, the world..." (Polar opposites, God and the world, brought together by love)... "That He gave His only begotten Son." I learned and saw firsthand in this multi-ethnic setting that the love of God is for OPPOSITES. It's a sacrificial giving of self for someone that is not like you. It is for someone that has not treated you the way you might have wanted to be treated. It is for those that don't look, act, think or live like you. When you learn to love those who are different from you and even those who mistreat you, you are walking in the love of God. When this happens, not only do you get out of you what's in you from God, but you get what God has for you from them. You become a new man, enabling you to accomplish more for God, more for others, and more for yourself. As I came into a diverse community of believers in that Bible College over twenty years ago, I began to receive a new heart, and when I did, I became a new man. I soon realized, as God began to open my understanding about His end-time purpose for the nations coming together in His house of prayer that I was sent by God into this ministry as a first fruits offering of the coming together of God's body in His house of prayer for all Nations. I was called to help prepare this church in my city to enter into reconciliation and the fullness of its calling. As I was given opportunities to grow in this ministry through serving, loving and speaking in this church's Bible College, I began to see my place in this community of believers. Over a period of ten years, spanning from the end of the twentieth century to the beginning of the twenty-first century, the racial landscape of this international mega-church in Columbus Ohio went from 5% African-American to 55% African-American.

Consequently, I came on staff at this church as its first African-American pulpit staff minister. The Caucasians and African-Americans within this ministry were completely integrated, thus positioning them to be reconciled to one another. This ministry became one of the foremost Christian ministries on the earth during that period. The scope of this ministry's reach went from a local outreach influence to a national and international reach, influencing this nation and the nations of the world. I watched this ministry's influence and affect in the world increase seemingly a hundredfold, as it embraced the nations and ethnic groups of the world. I believe I was sent into this ministry as a forerunner of the ministry of reconciliation to be a part of the establishing of the coming together of God's house of prayer for All Nations (Ethnicities). I was sent to help prepare this ministry to be prototype of what was coming in the twenty-first century; preparing His people for the coming of the Lord.

I believe God wants to raise up forerunners at the end of the age that take the message of reconciliation, fullness and the coming of the Lord to the nations of the world. I believe that just as during the era of the Civil Rights movement, African-Americans in American society must take the lead in this charge towards true reconciliation of all races in God's house. I believe we have a debt to pay to our forefathers and a responsibility to them to continue the fight for integration and reconciliation in our hearts in this generation, to make what they endured with their lives in their generation lasting and meaningful. Especially in the church of America, the one place where we should be integrated, Christians have a responsibility to come together across racial and ethnic lines to integrate and be reconciled, not only for the sake of past generations of freedom fighters, but for Jesus Christ, who died, was buried and rose again so that we would be one in Christ.

However, today, just like in Jesus' time when he visited the temple, and just like right before the Civil Rights movement, we have turned from a culture of prayer in our churches that brings together all races in Christ, to religion and the spirit of culturalism. We have turned to merchandising, corporate structuring, and entertainment in building the church of Jesus Christ, producing a culture of performance, competition and religious bigotry that further exacerbates the racial divide in the church. Therefore our churches are not being run by a dependency upon God in prayer, but primarily by manipulation, and control through the spirit of performance.

The 21st Century Plantation: The Religious Church

All of this, in addition to an elitist approach of relating in the church from the Clergy to the laity produces the same spirit of control behind racism that was at work during Slavery and Colonialism in the middle ages to control Africans on the plantations of their masters. This spirit of control behind racism, which is the spirit of superiority and domination of one people group over another, is actually what fuels the present system of religious, clergy hierarchy operating in the church today. This is actually what promotes and empowers the clergy and laity divisions and distinctions, which results in religious and ministerial bigotry, with our churches now becoming the Plantations, our Pastors our *Massa*, and His "so called members" the slaves for his vision. This spirit and system is one of the things which lead to

74

pervasive racism within the body of Christ. This is what divides and isolates churches, ministry gifts and people groups within the body of Christ.

This way of relating between the clergy and the laity within the Church of Jesus Christ was not seen when Jesus interacted with his disciples or with the common people he ministered to while on the earth in the first century church. This way of relating in religious circles has its root in this spirit of Leviathan – Pride, which was seen in how the Pharisees and religious leaders related with the common people during this same period of time. This Spirit of Leviathan is what produces this prideful religious and controlling spirit behind racism and bigotry in the church. This is the spirit that produces the superiority and domination in the church in how Pastors and Church leaders relate within their congregations. This is the spirit behind racism that must be broken for the body of Christ to come together in his house of prayer. This spirit that is the root of racism keeps people from truly hearing from God and obeying the spirit of God to be and do all that God calls for a people, race or religious denominational groups in the earth. When the spirit of religion was broken over my life I was set free from a bondage that I didn't know I was captive to. *I WAS SET FREE, AND DIDN'T EVEN KNOW I WAS BOUND.* That's the subtlety of a religious spirit. You can be bound and not even realize you're in bondage.

The same spirit that Church leaders operate under to keep their congregants from going to another church, or listening to another pastor, is the spirit behind racism and bigotry – *Because I am who I am, I know best, I'm the most anointed, I'm the only one with the truth, etc, etc.* This spirit of Leviathan in religion produces a different type of slavery of the mind and heart, which is a relational, religious slavery. It is a slavery to a mindset of either, a false sense of superiority and domination, or a false sense of inferiority and low self esteem that is produced by fear, intimidation, and control of one people group over another. This spirit fosters bitterness, hatred, and un-forgiveness towards others that keeps people from relating with one another in love, faith and hope. In extreme religious settings the spirit of religion keeps people from completely and totally thinking for themselves. You are not allowed to do anything unless that leader says it's okay or gives his permission.

Within the operation of a Leviathan, religious spirit the attendants are not encouraged to take the initiative to do anything unless they are told to do so, or it is sanctioned by the leader. It's a hyper form of religious control that is bred through a misuse and abuse of the biblical doctrine of submission to authority. Though this doctrine is a legitimate doctrine in scripture, religious, controlling spirits within Christianity as well as the other major religions, misuse this doctrine to control and manipulate its people, and make the leader the know-all, be-all, do–no-wrong, everything that everyone's world within that religious group is to revolve around. It is a form of religious slavery of the minds of the people along the same lines of the plantation *"Massa"* and his slaves of the middle ages. This was how the Masters controlled their slaves during the era of slavery in the middle ages. Many plantation owners used the very scriptures of Jesus Christ to control and manipulate the slaves to keep them in voluntary bondage to their system of exploitation and domination. This type of religious spirit behind racism produces a psychological slavery that puts limitations on a person or people groups minds, holding them in shackles of inferiority to the ruling masses or persons against their will through manipulation, control, fear and intimidation. It keeps them in prescribed calculated boundaries that ultimately keep them from discovering and becoming who they were created to be, while never allowing them to leave a codependency on that leader or people group.

The Stronghold of a Religious Spirit

This stronghold – *the spirit of false Religion or a Leviathan, Religious spirit* - have kept many ethnic, people groups from God's full expression of who they are and from what God has called them to do. The religious tradition deals with a prescribed way of worshipping God that is legislated, regulated and passed down from those above, or from previous experiences or from previous generations. This spirit can become a major hindrance or obstacle, keeping people from a true, authentic encounter with God. It can even become a stronghold, keeping a person or people group in unidentifiable chains, right outside of a true relational experience with the true and living God.

The Breaking of Cultural and Religious Strongholds

It is dangerous when we allow these religious and cultural expressions to bind us in a culture that locks us outside of what God wants to do in the earth in bringing the races together. We can only come into the fruition of God's plan for our lives when we immerse ourselves in the diversity from the coming together with other races. In African-American Church presentations there's a strong emphasis on our emotional expression of the gospel. We have less emphasis on the Word of God and more emphasis on experiencing God in our emotions. A desire to experience God in our emotions, or feel God, is not wrong, it's who we are. However, when we fail to appreciate God's Word in our gospel presentation, we've allowed a cultural expression to bind us in African-American religious cultural-ism. When we fail to get any revelation from the sermons in our services, and go home not knowing what the preacher preached about, we are trapped in religious cultural-ism. If we feel like we just "had church" or "had a good service," but are not changed or pricked in our hearts, we've allowed a religious expression to bind us in African-American religious cultural-ism. When we've been in

77

church for five or ten years, yet still don't know the difference between the four gospels and the Pentateuch (5 books of Moses), we are bound in religious cultural-ism. As we position ourselves for a transition into God's house of prayer for all nations at the end of the age, we must realize that God doesn't have a Black church or a White church, a hispanic church, or an Asian Church, neither does God have a Jewish or Gentile Church. God only has one Church. It's the Church of God which is called the House of Prayer for all nations (ethnicities).

However, when you are in a particular region of the earth, what ever ethnicity or culture dominates that region, that's the predominant people group that will worship together in the church of that region. What will determine whether or not a cultural religious expression is a stronghold over a region or a people, holding them in that particular religious expression, is not the predominant people group represented in the Church of that region, but the mindset of that people group. When African-Americans are unable to appreciate any other cultural expressions of worship and sermon delivery in other church cultures there's a good chance there is a religious, cultural stronghold over that people. When African-Americans are unable to appreciate other church expressions like the African church or the Caucasian church as being an anointed service unless it is jumping and shouting and clapping on beats of 2 and 4, we've allowed a cultural expression to bind us in African-American religious culturalism. When we feel like we can't hear a sermon if the preacher is not performing, moaning and groaning, with a Hammond B3 organ backing him up, we've allowed a cultural expression to bind us in African-American religious culturalism. We must break down these walls in our churches that have kept us from coming out of our cultural expression into the larger Christian culture in the body of Christ. We must not remain segregated either by race, religion or culture in our churches. God is doing a new thing, and in this new thing within the end-time prayer movement in the earth, he's bringing the races together in his house of prayer for all nations. Many African-Americans have attempted to justify this continued leaning towards racial lines and cultural preferences and biases by pointing the finger at what our former oppressors did to us and what they still owe us. Many that do venture outside of our culture or our familiar religious *"All Black"* churches to intergrate into another culture or religious setting are labeled as either Uncle Toms, or those that are still attached to their former Masters from slavery. Many are labeled as trying to find their affirmation from assimilating into the white man's world. Many leaders in our churches justify this cultural leaning towards racial lines by stating that Caucasian leaders and parishoners have not shown a willingness to integrate into our societies, church circles or submit to our spiritual leadership in our churches or communities.

Whose Responsibility is it to Initiate Racial Reconciliation within the body

In the beginning of the church in the book of Acts God shows us who was to be the initiators of the reconciliation of the races within the body of Christ. At the initation of inclusion of the Gentiles into Christianity in Acts 10, it was not Peter or the Jewish leadership of the Christian Church that initiated their inclusion into salvation through faith in Jesus Christ. God had Cornelius initiate the hearing of the gospel through a visitation to Cornelius, the Italian Gentile. Then Cornelius sent his servants to Peter to call him to come to them to speak to them the message of Salvation.

> *Act 10:1-6 There was a certain man in Caesarea called Cornelius, a centurion of the band called the Italian band, 2 a devout man, and one that feared God with all his house, which gave much alms to the people, and prayed to God always. 3 He saw in*

*a vision evidently about the ninth hour of the day
an angel of God coming in to him, and saying unto
him, Cornelius.4 and when he looked on him, he
was afraid, and said, What is it, Lord? And he said
unto him, Thy prayers and thine alms are come up
for a memorial before God. 5 and now send men to
Joppa, and call for one Simon, whose surname is
Peter. 6 he lodges with one Simon a tanner, whose
house is by the sea side: he shall tell thee what thou
oughtest to do.*

The situation with the Gentile and Jewish Christians could easily be compared to our situation in race relations in the church today. The Gentiles were looked down on by Jews. The Jews thought they were better than the Gentiles, and treated the Gentiles as dogs. They were not allowed in the temple. They had a court outside the temple where they could come and pray if they converted to Judaism. And even there during Jesus' time, the courts of the Gentiles were being used to buy and sell animal sacrifices. The Jews felt they were the privileged class even though their land had been colonized by the Romans. They were not to have any dealings with the Gentiles.

God then releases his spirit upon them, in many ways affirming this belief within them, solidifying these attitudes based on the outpour of God's spirit on them in the upper room. In the midst of all of this God sends his angel to Cornelius to tell him to call the uppity Jew Peter, to come and speak at his house the message of Salvation. Cornelius sends his household servants to Peter to have him come and preach the gospel to them. Peter, as well as many Jews of that time, considered it repulsive to go into the house of any Gentile. They were considered dogs. However, when Cornelius' servants came to Peter, God had already dealt with Peter's prejudices and racists attitudes towards Gentiles in a dream on the roof of his house, enabling Peter to receive

Cornelius' servants, and the rest is history. Peter came and spoke to them the words of life. While he spake the spirit of the Lord fell on the Gentiles and they were baptized into the body of Christ right along side of their Jewish counterparts. If we are going to see the release of all that God has for us as Africans, African-Americans and the Diaspora we must come out of our box. African-American church Pastors must take the lead by inviting Caucasian Pastors, as well Asian, Jewish and all other races, to speak in their pulpits. We must recognize that it is incumbent upon us to seek out and look to integrate within the cultures and religious settings of our former oppressors in order to bring about reconciliation and fullness.

Prayer and Deliverance from Racism and the Spirit of Control

This is why the restoration of prayer, which produces a true encounter with Jesus, returning back to the church today is so needed. Jesus linked encounter prayer and deliverance from racism and religion when he said; *"My house shall be called of all nations, a house of prayer."* With this statement he was revealing what it would take to break the spirit of racism in the church. Where the prayer of encountering Christ is the culture of the house of God, man-made religion, and racism have no breeding ground. Where encounter prayer is the culture of the house of God the spirit of control and manipulation is not needed. When a spiritual leader prays and looks totally to God to build and lead the Church of Christ there's no need for control and manipulation to keep people in their place. God keeps them in their place, doing what He wants them to do in His Church as long as he wants them there, to accomplish His purposes and plans.

Encounter Prayer and the spirit of religion, (or a controlling spirit) operating in the church are antithetical operations. Wherever a people pray and encounter Jesus they ultimately make a choice to

81

let go of the controls. Either God's in control in the earth, through the prayers of man to God, inviting God's wisdom into His affairs to lead in governing the earth, or mans in control through manipulation and domination of other human beings because of prayerlessness, but never both. Wherever a people control they ultimately make the choice not to pray, or to pray less. That's why, I believe, there is very little leader sanctioned prayer meetings going on in the modern churches of the 21st century. You will either lead by God's control through encountering God in prayer, or by man's control through prayerlessness. When we choose the latter, we choose a culture that will inevitably lead to a climate that produces a ruling class, an underclass and racial, and/or clergy superiority and domination over people. This is so that those in the church or community will listen and do what they're told to do. When a spiritual leader teaches the church to pray and hear from God for themselves, he's ultimately teaching them to encounter God, and he becomes increasingly unnecessary in their lives. The more they learn to hear and know God the more they grow from a dependency on that leader to a dependency upon God. And consequently they become all that God created them to become.

What Runs Our Churches When We're Not a House of Prayer

As things stand today in the church there is little, to no encountering God prayer meetings being promoted or advocated in our church cultures and systems of operation in the modern church of the 21st century, thusly the racial divides in churches are based on the nationality of the leader. Because we don't run our churches by prayer; we run them by a man, and the systems he implements, our Churches are filled with controlling leaders. Why? because in the minds of many leaders to have a true encountering God prayer culture in our churches would be to lose control of those churches.

82

Many controlling leaders believe it would cause everybody to start hearing from God for themselves, aside from hearing Him through them, and cause them to begin coming together outside of their organized flow charts, to do what God tells them to do. People would start developing their own ministries and ministry initiatives that might threaten the supposed vision or direction of the church. The Pastor might lose allegiance of segments of the people to the churches vision, for their own visions. And ultimately what Pastors' fear the most; we might lose people to another man or woman's vision from within the church, to start their own church with "their" so-called members. Therefore we've learned how to run and operate our churches without congregational prophetic prayer meetings where the members encounter God for themselves. We've implemented systems that run our churches, both godly & ungodly systems; of performance, systems of faithfulness and reward, systems of competition and corporate posturing, systems of Clergy hierarchy, systems of administration and operation that are governed not by the spirit of God, through prayer, but by the spirit of manipulation, control and performance through man's wisdom and prayerlessness. This leads to a religious man-made system that leads to relational bondage in our churches. There is bondage with religious spirits that can even make the word of God preached in the church powerless to change lives. Before the word of God can become Spirit and life to a person, this spirit of religious tradition and culturalism has to be broken. Jesus said concerning the power of religious tradition;

> *Mar 7:9 And he said unto them, Full well do ye reject the commandment of God, that ye may keep your tradition 13... making void the word of God by your tradition, which ye have delivered: and many such like things ye do.*

The Forerunner Vision of Reconciliation to Unite the Races

In African-American circles God is wanting to bring his people out of this wilderness of institutionalized religiosity, to break us out of a spirit of religion that has produced a subtle and sometimes undetected reverse racists' mentality in our all Black Churches, that keeps us divided from other churches and races within the body of Christ and the nations. Reconciliation of brothers that have been offended cannot come through religious or governmental institutions or laws, but can only come when we encounter Jesus in prayer and wrestle with our carnal, sinful hearts and deal with our oppressive relational tactics we've used in relating with our brothers in Christ and the nations. This prayer of encounter prescription for reconciliation was seen in the life of Jacob and Esau's reconciliation in Genesis 32:22-32; 33:1-4

> *Gen 32:22 And Jacob rose up that night, and took his two wives, and his two women-servants, and his eleven sons, and passed over the ford Jabbok. 23 And he took them, and sent them over the brook, and sent over that he had. 24 And Jacob was left alone; and there wrestled a man with him until the breaking of the day. 25 And when he saw that he prevailed not against him, he touched the hollow of his thigh; and the hollow of Jacob's thigh was out of joint, as he wrestled with him. 26 And he said, Let me go, for the day breaks. And he said, I will not let thee go, except thou bless me. 27 And he said unto him, what is thy name? And he said, Jacob. 28 And he said, Thy name shall be called no more Jacob, but Israel: for as a prince hast thou power with God and with men, and hast prevailed.*

84

When Jacob encountered the angel of the Lord and wrestled with him til the breaking of day, he received a name change. This represented his heart and destiny being changed. His name was changed from Jacob, which means supplanter, deciever, trickster, to Israel, which means, *he will rule as God*. When we encounter Jesus in prayer we are changed from our carnal, sinful nature and given a new nature that empowers us to be reconciled with God and man. After Jacob was transformed through the encounter with the angel of God, he went forth to meet his brother, whose heart towards him had also been changed.

> *Gen 33:1 And Jacob lifted up his eyes, and looked, and, behold, Esau came, and with him four hundred men. And he divided the children unto Leah, and unto Rachel, and unto the two handmaids. 2 And he put the handmaids and their children foremost, and Leah and her children after, and Rachel and Joseph hindermost. 3 And he passed over before them, and bowed himself to the ground seven times, until he came near to his brother. 4 And Esau ran to meet him, and embraced him, and fell on his neck, and kissed him: and they wept.*

When was Esau's heart towards Jacob changed? I believe it was changed when Jacob encountered Jesus Christ (the Angel of the Lord) and wrestled with him til the breaking of day. When we encounter Christ in His house of prayer, God not only changes our hearts and destinies, he changes the hearts of our brothers and those close to us who's been at enmity with us. When we encounter Christ in prayer we will be delivered from a religious spirit and a spirit of Culturalism which has kept us divided and at odds with one another in the nations. In African- American circles we've allowed these two spirits – *Culturalism and Man-Made Religion* - to keep us segregated from the mainstream of what

God is doing in bringing the nations, people groups and cultures from all backgrounds together in one new man, within the body of Christ, making his house a house of prayer for all nations. I believe that the vision of the reconciliation of the races through the Christian Church was initiated and best articulated from the heart of God in the 20th century by Martin Luther King Jr, with his *I have a Dream speech in 1963*.

The Civil Rights movement was birthed out of the African-American Church, and it began the breaking down in our society in the U.S. and all over the world, of the legal walls of segregation and legislated racial discrimination. This enabled the races the opportunity to have access to one another for interaction and dialogue that was to lead to real reconciliation. However, even though we have passed through the era of civil rights and the breaking down of legal segregation in society in America, in our churches we are still segregated. Why? Because racism and discrimination cannot be eradicated with laws and legislations, because it didn't orginate there. It must be dealt with at its' roots – *the Church*, in order to get to the heart of man, which is accomplished by the Spirit of God. Because racsim hasn't been dealt with at its' roots, 50 years after the desegregation of public facilities in our nation, our churches are still the most segregated hour of the week. Lord deliver us from the spirit of the World and Leviathan that has produced false Religion and Racism.

Financial Collapse of Detroit of 2013

I believe that the Call solemn assembly prayer meeting for reconciliation and the African American Detroit clergy's failure to repent and forgive White America's history of racial oppression is connected the City of Detroit, in 2013, becoming the first major city in U.S. History to file for Bankruptcy. Cities of Refuge will only be built by overcoming the Pride of Leviathan that keeps the House of Prayer for all nations divided.

CHAPTER 5

7 STEPS TO PREPARING CITIES FOR THE COMING SYSTEMIC COLLAPSE

The Seven-Fold Process of Deliverance from the Spirit of Leviathan

I have heard of you by the hearing of the ear, but now my eye has seen you; Therefore, I despise myself, and I have repented on dust and ashes. Job 42:5, 6

From the book of Job there is a seven step process to being delivered from the Spirit of Leviathan, or the spirit of the world, preparing God's people for the coming systemic collapse and the Day of the Lord. Below are these seven steps. The next two chapters goes into detail on each process that God took Job through to be an intercessor for His generation.

1. The Death of Loss – Job 3-6
2. Ears to Hear & Eyes to See – (Understanding)– Job 42:1-5
3. Humility – (Denouncement of Prideful esteem of self confidence from achievement) - Job 42:6
4. True Repentance (Turning and returning to Jesus and His righteousness)– Job 42:6
5. Speak the truth about Jesus (what's been revealed during the process) – Job 42:8
6. Intercession for His friends (Prayer for the body of Christ to be delivered from the Spirit of Leviathan)– Job 42:7
7. Restoration of Wealth (transfer); of family, money, name, recognition, reputation, etc – Job 42:10

In Job 42:5, 6 we read the words of Job after he had come through the greatest trial of His life. Jobs life before the trial would seem to have been the ideal, most desirable life to have or live. In the beginning of the book of Job we are given a picture of the life of Job in Job 1:1-5.

> *There was a man in the land of Uz, his name was Job. And this man was perfect and upright, and fearing God, and turning away from evil. 2 And seven sons and three daughters were born to him.*
>
> *3 And his possessions were seven thousand sheep, and three thousand camels, and five hundred yoke of oxen, and five hundred she-asses, and a very great household, so that this man was greater than all the sons of the east.*
>
> *4 And his sons feasted in the house of each one on his day. And they sent and called their three sisters to eat and to drink with them.*
>
> *5 And it happened, when the day of feasting had gone around, Job would send and sanctify them. And he would rise early in the morning and offer burnt sacrifices according to all their number. For Job said, It may be that my sons have sinned, and cursed God in their hearts. This, Job always did.*

Job was perfect and upright, and feared God, and turned away from evil. The word, **"Perfect"** in the Hebrew text means "complete, pious or undefiled." The word **"Upright"** in the Hebrew text means to be righteous, and the Hebrew word for **"Fearing"** God, means to be morally reverent. So Job was complete, righteous and morally reverent. He had seven sons and three daughters. He possessed seven thousand sheep, three thousand camels, and five hundred yoke of oxen. He possessed five hundred she-asses, and a very great household, so that this man was greater than all the sons of the east. He regularly rose up early in the morning to pray and offer up sacrifice for his children to sanctify them in case they had sinned in their hearts.

Process # 1 - The Process of the Death of Loss

Job 1:21 Naked I came from my mother's womb, and naked I will depart. The Lord gave and the Lord has taken away; may the name of the Lord be praised.

In the midst of all of Job's piety, disciplined prayer life, and his faithfulness to eschew evil and fear God, God being petitioned and requisitioned of the Devil concerning the sons of God in the earth, actually recommended Job to Satan. God says in Job 1:7, 8;

Whence comest thou? Then Satan answered the LORD, and said, from going to and fro in the earth, and from walking up and down in it. 8 And the LORD said unto Satan, Hast thou considered my servant Job, that there is none like him in the earth, a perfect and an upright man, one that feareth God, and escheweth evil?

Satan was going to and fro in the earth, and walking up and down in it. The book of Job does not say what he was doing, but I Peter 5:8 tell us His Modus Operandi:

1Pe 5:8 Be sober, be vigilant; because your adversary the devil, as a roaring lion, walketh about, seeking whom he may devour:

89

From this verse we know Satan was looking for someone to devour. The word "devour" in the Hebrew text means to gulp down, to drink entirely. Satan was going throughout the earth looking for someone to consume, to gulp down, to totally devour, and God suggests to him Job, saying, *"Have you considered my servant Job, that there is none like him in the earth?* It's interesting that God would offer His servant that was perfect, upright, and feared Him, to Satan to be devoured. It tells us something about the process of God's making and shaping of who we are and what we are called to become and do. God actually leads us into the testing and trying of our person by the adversary in order that he may get us to all he has for us to become and to do.

We would look at Job's life and figure that his life is the ultimate life and place in God, however God sees different than we do. He's trying to get us to Christ-likeness, not to comfort, wealth and material or familial blessing. The ultimate expression of Christ-likeness is when we like Jesus, getting ready to be crucified for the sins of the world, say, *"Father let this cup (trial) pass from me, Nevertheless, Not my will, but thine will be done.* The father was after the sacrificial offering up of His Son, for the reconciling of the world to God. Christ was willing to be beaten, scourged, spit on, forsaken by God and Man and killed on a cruel rugged Cross in order to reconcile the world back to God. God is after getting the world reconciled to Him from the spirit of Leviathan, through the sacrifice of our lives to Him, that we may have eternal access to the throne for His purposes in the earth. His goal for our lives is not that we would be perfect, upright or God fearing. Those characteristics are means to the end of the ultimate sacrifice of our lives to Him for eternal access to the father for intercession unto reconciliation of the world to God

The end of God's mark for our lives is that we would become Sons of God, mature to receive the inheritance of Son-ship. The inheritance of son-ship is eternal access that comes through sacrifice. God's goal for our lives is that we would come into his presence as Sons of God, going to and fro into the earth as High Priests.

Job 1:6 Now there was a day when the sons of God came to present themselves before the LORD, and Satan came also among them.

God's plan for Job was promotion to Christ-likeness. This process of getting us to the place and posture of Christ-likeness as a Son of God through great tribulation and persecution from the devil should not be a foreign process to the believer in Christ. It is not only seen in how God offered up Job to Satan to be purged and purified to come into His presence, but it was also seen in the New Testament in how Jesus was led of the Spirit into the wilderness to be tempted of the Devil in Matthew 4, and Luke 4, as well as when Jesus offered up Peter to Satan to be sifted as wheat in Luke 22.

Mat 4:1 then was Jesus led up of the Spirit into the wilderness to be tempted of the devil.

Luk 4:1 and Jesus being full of the Holy Ghost returned from Jordan, and was led by the Spirit into the wilderness, 2 Being forty days tempted of the devil.

Luk 22:31 And the Lord said, Simon, Simon, behold, Satan hath desired to have you, that he may sift you as wheat: 32 But I have prayed for thee, that thy faith fail not: and when thou art converted, strengthen thy brethren.

The Seasons of Satan

There are seasons of Satan in our lives, where the Lord will actually give the devil permission to come into our lives and tempt us, to reveal to us who we are and what's in us. The Lord will not tempt us with evil, but he will grant Satan permission to do so, in order to sift us as wheat. He will use the devil and his temptations, attacks and persecutions to get us to the place of recognition of who we really are, and what we're really made of, so that we can despise ourselves outside of Him, and truly repent in sackcloth and ashes, turning from a dependency upon self and our flesh to a dependency upon God through Jesus Christ.

This is where Jesus led Peter, after Satan sifted Him as wheat, and he ended up denying that he ever knew Jesus. Peter was at a place where he would realize that without Christ he was nothing, and nobody. But after he recognized who he was and who he wasn't he was a candidate to receive the power of the Holy Ghost on the day of Pentecost to make Peter what he couldn't be on his own. This was also what happened to Job after His most severe testing and trial at the hands of Satan. It caused him to search after who he really was, by searching after who God really was. Job said in Job 42:5, 6;

> *I have heard of thee by the hearing of the ear: but now mine eye seeth thee. 6 Wherefore I abhor myself, and repent in dust and ashes.*

Without the seasons of Satan released into our lives at the permission of God to reveal to us just how detestable we are, (not to God, but to us), we will not truly repent of our lives, which is the essence of the sin nature that makes up how we were born, and turn from that life to the life of Christ. We, like Job, will think our lives are okay. We will think, we just need to do our daily penance, for us and for our family and God will continue to cover us and bless us. But what about when we're doing all of that and tragedy hits our lives, or our family? Would we get offended and curse God and die? Are we doing our little religious daily penance to procure God's blessing for us, or are we seeking God for His will for our lives, whatever it may be, good or bad? Jesus lived His life with the realization that it would be filled with good and bad, victories and seeming defeat, blessings and suffering. Jesus spoke these words in Luke 9:21 to His disciples concerning the destiny of His life and ministry.

> *Luk 9:21 And he straitly charged them, and commanded them to tell no man that thing; 22 Saying, The Son of man must suffer many things, and be rejected of the elders and chief priests and scribes, and be slain, and be raised the third day.*

Many believers have faith to keep away the bad in their lives, but few develop their faith to go through the bad in their life. Many believers pray to avoid the sin, but few pray to be able to stand and continue in God's will for our lives in the midst of the struggle with sin. This is how the 21st century believer attends church, to get forgiven, or to feel better about ourselves (our sinful nature), or to receive God's blessing on our lives and family. We may repent of our sins, because we know our sins need to be repented of. But it ends up being a shallow repentance without any hope of true lasting deliverance. This is because many do not recognize that their whole life and how we approach life, from our selfish, sinful lens of life in the world system needs to be repented of.

The very essence of life as we know it in this world system and who we are in this world needs to be repented of. What we do, what we act out in our lives, what we pursue and what we set as our goals in life are all the results of the spirit of Leviathan - spirit of the world – lust of the eye, lust of the flesh and pride of life. This makes up the very essence of who we are. This is what needs to be repented of, not just what we do – the acts of sin. The very essence of who we are comes from a combination of these and several other different dynamics, and it all needs to be repented of, not just our sinful acts. The whole sinful system that makes up who and what we've become in our world must be repented of.

Process #2 - The Process of Developing Ears to Hear Eyes to See– Job 42:5

*I have heard of You by the hearing of the ear, but
now my eye has seen You*

Job's process after he lost everything took him to a desperate need to hear from God concerning what he was going through. Much of what Job was hearing from His friends was shallow, circumstantial surmising based on Job's loss. After hearing from His friends and yet not having received sufficient revelation of what He was going through and why, Job began to get real with God and talk to God for himself with a frankness and desperateness that required a response from God.

Learning to hear from God for ourselves produces personal encounters

Hearing from and seeing the glorified Christ is going to be vital to being prepared for the coming of the Lord. Hearing from and seeing the glorified Christ is going to be vital to restoring prayer that encounters the Glorified Christ back to its rightful place in the body of Christ. Notice, after Job had enough of listening to his friends on why he was going through what he was going through, he begin to seek and hear from God for Himself. **In order to seek God for ourselves, we must learn to hear from God for ourselves.** When you can't hear from God for yourself, you don't pray when you need God, you go looking for someone to pray for you, someone you think can get a prayer through. The problem with that is you might end up getting Job's friends as your prayer partner. When you can't hear from God for yourself, you don't pray when you need God, you go looking for someone to preach you a sermon or someone to give you a word. The problem with that is you might end up getting the sermons preached over your life that Job's friends preached over him, which God himself told

94

Job's friends, were not the truth concerning Him. None of the things that Job's friends surmised about Job's situation were why Job was suffering what he was suffering.

If we are unable to hear from God or if we are unable to scale the mount of transfiguration and see Him we will become bored and unbelieving in our prayer life. That's where the 21st century church has found herself praying bored, apathetic prayers with no power and little results. Paul's prayer for the Ephesians Church will become increasingly necessary for the end-time church to pray, *"That the Father of glory would give unto the saints the spirit of wisdom & revelation in the knowledge of Jesus."*

Now my Eyes have seen you

Once Job sought the Lord for himself God showed Himself to Job, so that Job could say; *"I had heard of you before, but now my eyes have seen you, therefore I despise myself and repent in sackcloth and ashes."* As long as Job was hearing from God through His friends he was not compelled to repent of what he had become. There are some ways that we have that can't be readily seen on the surface of our lives. There are some ways that require an encounter with the Glorified Christ. If we continue hearing surface sermons that just tickle our ears, or messages that deal only with the leaves of sinful acts, but not with our sin nature, we will never get to a place where we truly repent of the very nature and ways of man in the earth, that keep us from seeing Jesus and becoming like Him.

I saw the Lord High and Lifted Up

When Job saw the Lord, he would be challenged and empowered to turn from Adam – his sin nature, to Jesus, God's righteousness nature - in order to turn from his essence to God's very essence as the son of God. What was it that caused Job to abhor himself? The scripture says that Job had seen the Lord. Job said, I had heard about

95

you with the hearing ear, but now MY EYE HAS SEEN YOU, WHEREFORE I ABHOR MYSELF. *Job had to first see what his life was supposed to be before he could turn from what his life had become.* This is the beholding, becoming principle of deliverance in scripture found in I Corinthians 3:18. *But we all, with open face beholding as in a glass the glory of the Lord, are changed into the same image from glory to glory, even as by the Spirit of the Lord.* This was also what happened to Isaiah in Isaiah 6:1-5

> *In the year that king Uzziah died I saw also the Lord sitting upon a throne, high and lifted up, and his train filled the temple. 2 Above it stood the seraphims: each one had six wings; with twain he covered his face, and with twain he covered his feet, and with twain he did fly. 3 And one cried unto another, and said, Holy, holy, holy, is the LORD of hosts: the whole earth is full of his glory. 4 And the posts of the door moved at the voice of him that cried, and the house was filled with smoke. 5 Then said I, Woe is me! for I am undone; because I am a man of unclean lips, and I dwell in the midst of a people of unclean lips: for mine eyes have seen the King, the LORD of hosts.*

Once Isaiah saw the Lord in all of His holiness and glory he was able to see how undone He was and how undone His generation was. It was then that God released the fire off the altar to touch His lips to purge him of his sinfulness, or his sinful nature.

> *Isa 6:6 Then flew one of the seraphims unto me, having a live coal in his hand, which he had taken with the tongs from off the altar: 7 And he laid it upon my mouth, and said, Lo, this hath touched thy*

lips; and thine iniquity is taken away, and thy sin purged.

Notice when Isaiah saw the Lord, and saw His sinful nature, the Angel that laid the fire from the altar on His mouth, took away his iniquity, not just his sins. His iniquity represents generational sins passed down, not just his sins he committed. The sins that were a part of His generational make-up were taken away first, and His sins, those acts that he was committing, were then purged. This is also what Job experienced when he saw the Lord. He abhorred himself and turned from His generational sins, as well as his personal sins.

Process # 3 - The Process of Humility

Therefore, I despise myself, and I have repented on dust and ashes. Job 42:5, 6

Once you come to the place, like Isaiah, and Job, where you see Jesus, you are humbled in the presence of God, seeing the utter wretchedness of your sinful nature. It was not until Job was able to see through all the surface good deeds and material and relational success he had achieved, through to the wretchedness that was at the core of his life, that he was able, in Humility, to despise what he had become and humble himself and repent in sackcloth and ashes. This type of repentance is a season of repentance from a place of consecration and set aside time with the Lord. This type of repentance is not a quick fix time of repentance to deal with a surface act of sin, but a season of seeking and searching for God's plan, purpose and will that has yet to be revealed. This type of repentance requires a Humility that says, what I thought I knew about God and His will for my life I now realize I don't know.

Humble Thyself through Fasting

How does one humble himself? Psalms 35: 13 *says, I humbled myself through fasting; and my prayer returned into mine own bosom.* Matt 18:4 *Whosoever therefore shall humble himself as this little child, the same is greatest in the kingdom of heaven.*

1. One way to humble your self is through prayer and fasting.

Fasting is part of the normal Christian life. It is often thought of as an optional discipline. Jesus said, *"When you fast,"* implying that it should occur in the regular course of a disciple's life.

> *[17]When you fast...[18]your Father who sees in secret will reward you openly. (Mt. 6:17-18)*

Jesus emphasized that the Father **will reward** fasting. This proclamation makes fasting important. Jesus called us to fast because He knows that its rewards will far outweigh its difficulties. Some of the rewards are **external**, as our circumstances are touched by God's power. Some of our rewards are **internal**, as our hearts encounter Him. We fast both to walk in more of God's power to change the world, and to encounter more of His heart to change our heart!

God gives grace to fast. If we ask for grace to fast we will receive it (2 Pet. 1:2; 3:18). Many fear fasting. However, the fear of fasting is worse than fasting itself. It is a lie that the demands of our modern pace of life make fasting impractical for today's Christian.

Throughout history, men have fasted with a wrong spirit as they sought to earn God's favor or man's approval. Some embrace extreme self-debasements to try to prove their dedication to Him or to earn His favor. We do not fast to prove anything to God or to deserve His favor.

Many who led the great revivals practiced regular fasting. Examples include John Wesley, George Whitefield, Jonathan Edwards, David Brainerd, and Charles Finney. Wesley fasted on Wednesdays and Fridays each week and insisted that all the preachers under him do the same

2. Another way to humble your self is by placing yourself under a man or woman to learn and receive what they have, or what they know, to do what you need to do.

   I Peter 5: 5, 6 says, Likewise, ye younger, submit yourselves unto the elder. Yea, all of you be subject one to another, be clothed with humility: for God resists the proud, and gives grace to the humble. Humble yourselves therefore under the mighty hand of God, that he may exalt you in due time:

Submission is a sign of humility. In order to humble yourself you have to voluntarily submit to God-ordained authority. To humble yourself under the mighty hand of God is to submit to the governmental authority of the five fold ministry gifts within the Body of Christ. Those ministry gifts are; The Apostle, Prophet, Evangelist, Pastor, Teacher. These are listed in Ephesians 4:11. When we submit to the mighty hand of God He will exalt us in due time. However, we are not able to submit on our own, neither are we commanded to submit on our own. We are commanded to first humble ourselves. Once we humble ourselves we can receive the grace to submit ourselves.

   James 4:6-7 says, But he gives more grace. Wherefore he saith, God resists the proud, but he gives grace unto the humble. Submit yourselves therefore to God. Resist the devil, and he will flee from you. Draw nigh to God and he will draw nigh to you.

One of the things that cause us to be able to resist the temptations of the devil is our submission to God-ordained authority. When we don't submit to God-ordained authority we will not be able to resist the devil. (James 4:7...*Submit yourselves to God, resist the devil, and he will flee from you).*

God-Ordained Authority

What is God-ordained authority? It is the authority of the family. It is the authority of the church, the five-fold gift ministries. It is the authority of government, the laws of the land.

> Romans 13:1 *Let every soul be subject unto the higher powers. For there is no power but of God: the powers that be are ordained of God. Whosoever therefore resists the power, resists the ordinance of God; and they that resist shall receive to themselves damnation.*

> Ephesians 5:21, 22 *Submitting yourselves one to another in the fear of God. Wives submit yourselves unto your own husbands, as unto the LORD.*

> James 5:5 *Likewise, ye younger, submit yourselves unto the elder. Yea, all of you be subject one to another, and be clothed with humility: for God resists the proud, and gives grace to the humble.*

The power to submit comes from the grace of God. *He gives more grace. Wherefore he saith, God resists the proud, but gives grace to the humble.*

Grace is the power of God working on your behalf without you earning it, qualifying for it, or working for it. It is the unmerited favor of God. It is the divine enabling of God. Grace is God doing for you what you could not do for yourself. In order to receive this grace we must first seek it, find it and receive it by faith.

> Ephesians 2:8, 9 *for by grace are ye saved through faith; and that not of yourselves: it is the gift of God: Not of works, lest any man should boast.*

Grace is a gift that comes from God. It is something that is bestowed upon us by the favor of God. And it enables us to work for him, live for him and obey his word. It is received by faith, but it requires our seeking after it. *For by grace are ye saved through faith.* But even though it is received by faith it also must be found. Hebrews 4:16 *Let us therefore come boldly unto the throne of grace, that we may obtain mercy, and find grace to help in the time of need.* A person that is humble is one that is quick to respond to and obey the spirit of God, and is easily led by God's Spirit and by man.

Humility and a Culture of Honor

It is important that we honor others in pursuing the ministry of the Spirit and do not yield to an elite spirit. We love God by honoring all the people that He calls and who are dear to Him.

The Spirit requires that we dwell together in a ***culture of honor***. God's blessing flows when we honor others. The Spirit desires to establish a culture of honor and humility in His kingdom. We must honor the whole Body of Christ and the work of the Spirit in all the different streams of the Body (Baptist, Nazarene, Presbyterian, Anglican, Episcopal, Charismatic, Catholic, etc.)

101

We must have a deep sense of our need for others, along with a sense of the inadequacies and shortcomings in our own life and ministry. It is not okay to be removed or isolated from others. Born-again believers who agree on the *main and plain issues of faith* <u>must walk in a spirit of honor</u>, even while disagreeing about various ministry values and focuses.

The main and plain issues of faith include salvation by faith, the authority of Scripture, walking out the two great commandments, evangelizing the lost, and working to transform our cities and disciple nations. When we humble ourselves and turn from our selfish, carnal works and see ourselves as wretched outside of God, we can return to God with a repentant heart, freeing ourselves from the Spirit of Leviathan - the spirit of this world, of the lust of the flesh, lust of the eye and the pride of life. In the next chapter we will continue the 7 step process to being delivered from the Spirit of Leviathan, and being prepared for the coming systemic collapse.

CHAPTER 6

THE SEVEN-FOLD PROCESS OF DELIVERANCE FROM THE SPIRIT OF LEVIATHAN – *Continued – Process #4-7*

Therefore, I despise myself, and I have repented on dust and ashes. Job 42:5, 6

Process # 4 - The Process of True Repentance

Without these seasons where God processes us we will not repent truly of who we are, or what we've become. We will continue to only repent of what we've done. This type of repentance, of what we do, can never accomplish lasting deliverance from the Spirit of Leviathan. This type of repentance is a shallow, head repentance, rather than deep heart repentance. This type of repentance is a repentance that comes from specific actions rather than from the roots of those actions, which is our carnal sinful nature and the spirit of the world.

Repentance in Sackcloth & Ashes

As was stated in the previous Chapter, it wasn't until Job abhorred himself that he could really repent in sackcloth and ashes. Up until then, Job was focusing and concentrating on his and his children's actions. He was repenting for himself and his children for what they did, or what they might do. These religious acts revealed where Job's mindset was concerning deliverance. He had consigned that he and his family would always be bound to the proclivities and propensities of sin, so the only hope was to schedule regular times of sacrifice to take care of all the sins we know we're bound to commit. It says in Job 1:5;

> *5 And it happened, when the day of feasting had gone around, Job would send and sanctify them. And he would rise early in the morning and offer burnt sacrifices according to all their number. For Job said, It may be that my sons have sinned, and cursed God in their hearts. This, Job always did.*

Job had to get to the place where he went from repenting from his and his children's actions to repenting for who he was. He had to go from repenting for actions to repenting for the very sin nature (Adamic nature) that produced the actions. To get to that place where he repented for who he had become in his self-nature, which is rooted in the sin nature, he was going to have to see God in a way that he had never seen him before. He was going to have to see him in a way that he would see who he was supposed to be in Christ before the Adamic nature of sin set in - "...*I had heard of you before, but now my eyes have seen you. (Job 42:5).*

The problem in us not repenting of our nature of sin is that we are not pursuing Christ-likeness. We measure ourselves by ourselves, or by others that we consider are worse off than we are. Instead of us pursuing Christ-likeness, and realizing that Jesus is the standard, not someone or something else, we measure ourselves entirely by man's standard of righteousness and performance. This is all as a result of our faulty understanding of the process to Christ-likeness.

Why Repent

In the Church we have preached repentance to miss hell and make it to heaven. Or we have preached repentance from sin only. However, we can see from Acts 3:19, 20 that repentance ultimate aim is Jesus. Repentance is the process back to Christ-likeness;

*19 **Repent ye therefore, and be converted,** that your sins may be blotted out, when the times of refreshing shall come from the presence of the Lord; 20 **And he shall send Jesus Christ,** which before was preached unto you:*

With repentance being the process to Christ-likeness, repentance becomes a way of life, not just something we do when we commit sinful acts. We don't repent because we've sinned; we repent because we have not yet arrived at Christ-likeness. You repent because you are still more like you than you are like Him.

To Repent Requires the Word of God

The word *"Repent"* means to re-think, or to have or consider another thought. The word re-pent is a combination of two words. The first word is "Re"- means to do again. The second word is "Pent"- which means to think, or a thought. You might recognize better the thought process behind the word Re-Pent by another word that the suffix "Pent" is used in – *Pent-house*. The top floor of a high rise building is called the Penthouse. Therefore to repent is to think again your situation, or to come back to life lived on top. It is to turn from one thought to God's higher thought. It means to come back again to life lived with the Spirit of God on top, leading your flesh, not following your carnal desires.

Therefore, you don't necessarily have to have committed an act of sin to repent. You just have to look in the word of God and get a thought from God that's not your thought. When this happens, and you allow the Spirit of God to turn you from your thoughts to God's thoughts you have just repented.

Jobs Good Works could not Deal with His Iniquities

Once Satan was released to attack all that Job had, all of his religious acts and sacrifices no longer made sense. Job's religious works were not working. His children were killed, his property was destroyed, and His body was afflicted. All Job had was now gone. Job 1:12-19

Once all Job had was gone, Job arose and rent his mantle, and shaved his head, and fell down upon the ground and worshipped. However, this still did not translate into Job repenting from who he had become. Job was not at that place of true repentance yet. The scripture says, that Job fell down and worshipped, but it didn't say that he repented. Job did not realize that he needed to repent yet. Job's worship was still a part of his religious act. He could not worship from His heart yet, nor truly repent yet, because Job had yet to see the Lord, therefore had he yet to see his sinful nature. His sinful nature was shrouded over by his religious works. Job still needed more revelation of God and himself before he could worship from His heart and repent truly of who he was, and not just for what he would do. So he began asking God questions, because he could not understand what was going on. He was praying and keeping Himself from acts of sin, and his life was still attacked by death, tragedy and loss of property. Neither he, nor his wife could understand why his life was attacked when he was not committing evil, sinful acts. God doesn't just want us to be delivered from the acts of sin that we commit, but from the very desire and propensity for those sins we commit. God doesn't want to change us from the outside in, but from the inside out.

In order for Job to repent and worship God in spirit and truth, Job's nature and what he was, was going to have to be abhorred, even when his actions were right. Even when our actions are righteous, our lives are still unrighteous outside of Christ, because our righteousness is filthy rags to Him.

Process #5 - The Process of the Truth about who Jesus is and the spirit of Leviathan

Job 42:7 The LORD said to Eliphaz: What my servant Job has said about me is true, but I am angry at you and your two friends for not telling the truth.

After Job had seen the Lord and began to understand what was happening unto him, Job was able to see his situation through the eyes of God. He began to receive truth about the awesomeness and weightiness of who God really was. Jobs friends, however, did not speak the truth of the nature and character of God in Job's situation. As a result God required Job's friends to go to Job so that Job could pray for them. When we fail to see God for ourselves we come short of the Glory of God. When we fail to see who God is for ourselves we come short of the truth necessary to set us free from Satan, sin and the Spirit of the world.

John 14:6 *"I am the Way, the Truth and the Life."*

JESUS CHRIST was and is the Truth about God. He said in John 14:6, *"I am the way,"* but to what? What was Jesus referring to when he said I am the way? Thomas had just asked, "Show us the father," Jesus first replied by saying when you've seen me you've seen the father. He then replied by saying I am the way to the father. What Jesus was emphasizing to his disciples from this verse is that the way to access the father is found through three simple truths made clear by Jesus' statement, *"I am the Way, the Truth and the Life."*

1. Jesus came first to show us the way to access the father through his forerunner ministry of going beyond the veil, tearing down the middle wall of partition, to give us access to a relationship with

our heavenly father. This would cause us to see him for ourselves within ourselves.

2. He secondly came to lead us to the truth of who the father was,
3. And lastly He came to lead us into this way of access as an eternal lifestyle. *I am the Way, the Truth, and the Life.*

Only the one who has gone ahead of us can show us the way. He came first to make a way for us to return to fullness, to access heaven and bring heaven to earth. I believe we've yet to scratch the surface in the church on what this way is that Jesus came to show us. We've known and stated correctly that Jesus is the way, but because we have known very little about the truth of who Jesus is and all that He represents and exemplifies to the believer, we've not been able to adequately articulate or walk out the way or ministry of Jesus Christ. If Jesus is the way, the truth and life, the believer that walks in this way should naturally go forth leading people to a relationship with Jesus with little to no effort because our encounter with others is preceded by our encounter with Jesus through intercessory prayer. It should be second nature. When we come to the understanding of Jesus Christ and the ministry of the forerunner we will lead people to the way that will prepare the people of the earth for the coming of the kingdom of God, and our eternal identity with him as Kings, and Priests.

Concerning his forerunner ministry In John 14:1 Jesus said;

> *"Let not your heart be troubled; you believe in God, believe also in me. In My father's house are many mansions; if it were not so, I would have told you. I go to prepare a place for you. And if I go and prepare a place for you, I will come again and receive you to myself; that where I am, there you*

108

may be also. And where I go you know, and way you know'

Hebrews 6:19-20 "This hope we have as an anchor of the soul, both sure and steadfast, and which enters the Presence behind the veil, where the forerunner has entered for us, even Jesus, having become High Priest forever according to the order of Melchizedek.

This is what Jesus was doing when He went to prepare a place for us; He was operating in this ministry. He was going before us to prepare the way for us to follow him. This is what Jesus was speaking of when he told his disciples, *"Where I am, there you may be also,"* and *"Where I go you know and the way you know."* He was speaking of going behind the veil to open up the way for all humanity to have access to the Father as priests, just as he had. He was going before us as a FORERUNNER to make way for us to fulfill our ministry as kings and priests in the earth.

Jesus gives us all Power in Heaven and Earth over the Spirit of Leviathan

When Job was encountered by God, we are introduced to the subject and purpose of Job's process – *The Spirit of Leviathan and the Christ-like nature that's necessary to defeat the spirit of Leviathan.* In Job 38-41 we are introduced to the Spirit of Leviathan, as God begins to question Job, asking; "Where were you when I created the heavens and the earth." This dialogue with Job about Leviathan seems inappropriate or out of place unless we realize what Jobs trial is all about. Job's trial was actually all about the process necessary to overcome and be delivered from the spirit of Leviathan, or the spirit of the world. God questions Job as to how easily He created the earth, and how easily He was able to deal with Leviathan, while asking Him how he would fare against Leviathan. He scolds Job, as

He then states, (*In my own vernacular and scripture version*) if you cannot stand up to Leviathan, How dare you question me about the process I take you through to be freed from Leviathan, and to be able to free others from this spirit. If you, in the state you were in, could not stand before Leviathan, how dare you stand before me questioning me about the process I've taken you through to get you delivered from Leviathan? He states the ease by which God dispatches and dispels the Spirit of Leviathan, and compares how he deals with this monster in the earth, with man's, and his inability to be free from this spirit or even confront this spirit on his own.

Job 41:1 Canst thou draw out leviathan with an hook? or his tongue with a cord which thou lettest down? 2 Canst thou put an hook into his nose? or bore his jaw through with a thorn? 3 Will he make many supplications unto thee? will he speak soft words unto thee?

4 Will he make a covenant with thee? wilt thou take him for a servant forever? 5 Wilt thou play with him as with a bird? or wilt thou bind him for thy maidens?

6 Shall the companions make a banquet of him? shall they part him among the merchants? 7 Canst thou fill his skin with barbed irons? or his head with fish spears? 8 Lay thine hand upon him, remember the battle, do no more.

9 Behold, the hope of him is in vain: shall not one be cast down even at the sight of him? 10 None is so fierce that dare stir him up: who then is able to stand before me?

11 Who hath prevented me that I should repay him? whatsoever is under the whole heaven is mine. 12 I will not conceal his parts, nor his power, nor his comely proportion.

In this, God not only gives Job a revelation of the awesomeness of God and the power and ease by which He dispatches the fiercest enemies of God and man, but He also gives Job a revelation of the purpose of Job's process of the death of Loss and the purpose of God for His life – *Freedom from the Spirit of Leviathan in the earth, as well as the deliverance of His friends and family from this spirit through his (Job's) intercessory prayer ministry.*

Job 42:8 So I want you to go over to Job and offer seven bulls and seven goats on an altar as a sacrifice to please me. After this, Job will pray, and I will agree not to punish you for your foolishness. 9 Eliphaz, Bildad, and Zophar obeyed the LORD, and he answered Job's prayer. 10 After Job had prayed for his three friends, the LORD made Job twice as rich as he had been before.

Process #6 - Intercessory Prayer for family and friends

(Praying for the body of Christ to be delivered from the Spirit of Leviathan) – Job 42:7

After this, Job will pray, and I will agree not to punish you for your foolishness Job 42:7

Before the return of His Son, the Father has determined that the Body of Christ will be described as a *praying Church* and the bowls containing the prayers of the saints will be full—unlike any time in history. The Lord has scheduled a prayer movement that will sweep the entire planet in the generation that the Lord returns.

111

There will be a unified cry of intercession from the Body of Christ at the end of the age, saying; *Come Lord Jesus, the Spirit and the Bride say COME* - (Isaiah 56:5-8; 61:11-62:1, 6,7; Zech. 8:18-22; 12:10; 1 Chr. 9:33; Lev. 6:12-14; 24:2-4; Rev. 12:10; 1 Thess. 3:10; 1 Tim. 5:5; Rev. 5:8; Ps. 134:1; 135: 1-3). *God demands that this "cry of intercession" be in place before He sends His Son.* Jesus' Return will not happen *except in response* to the cry of the praying church.

In order for the church to pray for the return of Christ, we must be delivered from the spirit of the world that is Anti-Christ. This is what Job was being delivered from through this process of loss, or death to self, the Spirit of Leviathan. He was being made an intercessor to pray for His friends, family and their deliverance from this same spirit. The Praying Church must understand the spirit that's holding back the fullness of God's Spirit from being released in the earth, and she must understand the spirit of Intercession being released as we are delivered from the spirit of the world.

What is intercession?

Intercession is intimate partnership and agreement with God.
1. Intercession is intimacy. Prayer is an exchange of romance. God speaks to us and it moves our hearts. When we speak back to God, His heart is moved. God desires to establish or deepen this romantic relationship with us. He desires intimacy with us. He wants us to know His heart and more so, to feel the very emotions of His heart, and then He wants to hear us cry out for the longings of His heart to come to pass. His longings become our longings. It's partnership at the most intimate level possible. We begin to feel and do what God feels and does. *"For Zion's sake I WILL NOT HOLD MY PEACE, and for Jerusalem's sake I WILL NOT REST..."(Isaiah 62:1)"I have set watchmen on your walls, O Jerusalem; THEY SHALL NEVER HOLD THEIR PEACE day or night.*

You who make mention of the Lord, do not keep silent, and GIVE HIM NO REST..."(Isaiah 62:6)

2. Intercession is partnership. Intercession is the means by which God's will is established on earth. God does not act apart from human beings partnering with His heart. Intercession expresses the bridal identity of the church. There is nothing more powerful that can fuel God's heart to move upon the earth than the cry of His bride, whose desires reflect His own.

3. Intercession is agreement with God. Intercession is agreement with what God promised to do. When we ask God to do what He desires to do, we are declaring that we agree that His desires are good, and that His desires have become our desires.

Intercession Expresses God's Definition of the Church

"...My house shall be called a HOUSE OF PRAYER for all nations."(Isaiah 56:7)

"...PRAYER ALSO WILL BE MADE FOR HIM (JESUS) CONTINUALLY, and daily He shall be praised."(Psalm 72:15)

"PRAY WITHOUT CEASING..."(1 Thessalonians 5:17)

Process #7 – The Restoration of Wealth (transfer); of family, money, name, recognition, reputation, etc

Job 42:10 And the LORD turned the captivity of Job, when he prayed for his friends: also the LORD gave Job twice as much as he had before. 11 Then came there unto him all his brethren, and all his sisters, and all they that had been of his acquaintance

> *before, and did eat bread with him in his house:*
> *and they bemoaned him, and comforted him over*
> *all the evil that the LORD had brought upon him:*
> *every man also gave him a piece of money, and*
> *everyone an earring of gold. 12 So the LORD*
> *blessed the latter end of Job more than his*
> *beginning: for he had fourteen thousand sheep,*
> *and six thousand camels, and a thousand yoke of*
> *oxen, and a thousand she asses.*

When Job prayed for His friends to be delivered from this same spirit of Leviathan, God restored Job's fortunes, and gave Him twice as much as he had before. As the church becomes a House of Prayer and develops Cities of refuge God is going to release a wealth transfer to the Church that causes the Church to thrive, not just survive, during the most economically trying times in all of human history.

Over the last several years I believe God has been judging and shaking the church (believers), processing us as he did Job's life to get us to the place where we're free from the Spirit of the World, (Flesh, Lust and Pride) so that we can handle all the money God wants to release to us and through us, for His kingdom at the end of the age.

> *1Pe 4:17 For the time is come that judgment must*
> *begin at the house of God: and if it first begin at us,*
> *what shall the end be of them that obey not the*
> *gospel of God?*

Afterwards, I believe He will then judge and shake the world system as He did when Pharaoh refused to let the children of Israel go in the time of Moses' ministry. Just as God sent the ten plagues to cause Pharaoh to release his chosen people, God is going to send a shaking on this present world system. This

Judgment is going to cause his people to be shaken loose from their bondage and dependency upon the economic and financial system, in order to release a transfer of wealth from this system into the Church. God promised His people this transfer in scripture for the plundering of the kingdom of darkness and the building up of the kingdom of God.

Just as the children of Israel came out of Egypt with the wealth of Egypt, God is going to bring His church out of the world system with the wealth of the nations. The last thing to collapse before the children of Israel came out of Egypt was the Egyptian economy, as the Israelites demanded every one of his neighbors' jewels of gold and jewels of silver, as Moses had commanded them (Exodus 11:2, 3; 12 -35). As we see the beginnings of the coming collapse of the economic and financial systems in our nation and the nations of the world, we must also see this as a sign and an indication of God's desire to release wealth to His people. And as the people of God we must get in position, not only to be delivered from the spirit of Leviathan and come out of this system, but to have restored unto us double what we had before the process of loss, and arise with great wealth and power as we come out.

My Money is Restored

My Money is Restored is a book I wrote in 2010 from a word the Lord originally revealed to me in 1998, while I was reading the story of Joseph in Genesis 42:25-28.

> **Genesis 42:25-28** *Then Joseph commanded to fill their sacks with corn, and to restore every man's money into his sack, and to give them provision for the way: and thus did he unto them. And he laded their asses with corn, and departed thence. And as one of them opened his sack to give his ass*

115

provender in the inn, he espied his money; for, behold, it was in his sack's mouth. And he said unto his brethren, "MY MONEY IS RESTORED; AND, LO IT IS EVEN IN MY SACK."

It dawned on me that God wants to transition his people to restore, transfer and receive all the money that has been lost, unclaimed or stolen from His people as a consequence of oppressive economic and religious systems in the earth. There have been many things that God has restored in the earth since Adam's fall through the death burial and resurrection of Jesus Christ.

However, of all the restorations that have been brought back to the earth through Christ and His Church, one of the major and last things that must be restored to the body of Christ before Jesus returns is the abundance of money, wealth and resources in the church. Money, wealth and resources were a major part of the Pentecostal release of the spirit of God in the Book of Acts. Along with tongues, miracles, healing and supernatural deliverance, money was a part of the restoration of power and authority being given back to man in the earth. Money and resources within the church in Acts, being given by the people to the apostles, was one of the evidences that something supernatural had happened in the hearts of the believers as a result of the day of Pentecost outpouring. **Acts 4:32** records what happened financially and materially amongst the believers, when they had prayed for God to show himself with signs and wonders in the name of Jesus Christ. The place was shaken where they were gathered together.

And the multitude of them that believed were of one heart and of one soul: neither said of them that aught of the things which he possessed was his own; but they had all things in common. And with great power gave the apostles witness of the

116

resurrection of the Lord Jesus Christ: and great grace was upon them all. Neither was there any among them that lacked: for as many as were possessors of lands or houses sold them, and brought the prices of the things that were sold,

And laid them down at the apostles feet: and distribution was made unto every man according as he had need.

And Joses, who by the apostles was surnamed Barnabas, a Levite, and of the country of Cyprus, <u>having land, sold it, and brought the money, and laid it at the apostles feet.</u>
(Acts 4:32)

These verses show us that money, wealth and resources within the context of the Christian community doing life together were a major part of the move of the spirit in the early church. And at the end of the age God is going to restore money, wealth and resources within the context of the church coming together in his house of prayer for all nations, to believe, have one heart and one soul, and to assure that there is none among us that lack. This restoration of money, wealth and resources is contingent upon the house of God once again becoming an international community of affection. Without community within the house of prayer to restore the money, wealth and resources of the church, the church will be unable to be all, do all, and complete all that God has commissioned her to do in the earth.

The Church presently in the year 2013 is in the midst of a process of purging, purifying and sifting, delivering her from the spirit of Leviathan, or the spirit of the World. She is in the midst of the decline of her wilderness seasons of loss, the burial of her past ways and man-made religious systems she obtained as a result of

117

doing ministry for temporal results, so that she might receive her resurrection of the Spirit of Revelation, Humility, True Repentance, Truth, Intercession and Wealth transfer to prepare the way of the earth for the coming of the Lord.

CHAPTER 7

COME OUT FROM AMONG THEM AND DON'T LOOK BACK

Gen 18:23-26 And Abraham drew near, and said, Wilt thou also destroy the righteous with the wicked?....And the LORD said, If I find in Sodom fifty righteous within the city, then I will spare all the place for their sakes.

Whenever God is determined to bring judgment on a region, he will always go looking for the righteous of that region, that he might show mercy and spare as many people as he can. The righteous are always the intercessors that stand between God and what he wants to do, and what He actually does. If he can find just a few righteous in a city He will spare that city for the righteous sake. However, once He has determined that the city is going to be judged because of the wickedness of that city, the righteous have a decision to make. They can come out of the sins of that city and escape the judgment, or they can continue in the sins of that city and receive the same judgment that the unrighteous receive. As was the case with Sodom and Gomorrah, such will be the case with the body of Christ in the last generation.

Luk 17:26 And as it was in the days of Noe, so shall it be also in the days of the Son of man. 27 They did eat, they drank, they married wives, they were given in marriage, until the day that Noe entered into the ark, and the flood came, and destroyed them all. 28 Likewise also as it was in the days of Lot; they did eat, they drank, they bought, they

119

> *sold, they planted, they builded; 29 But the same day that Lot went out of Sodom it rained fire and brimstone from heaven, and destroyed them all. 30 Even thus shall it be in the day when the Son of man is revealed.*

We have come to a very a critical time in the church in our nation. We must decide what we're going to stand for, what we're going to believe and how we're going to live. There are times when those decisions can be filled with shades of grey and we get by. There are times when those decisions can be delayed or even denied as we live in a time or season of compromise, not being fully committed to God or his principles, and not being totally sold out to the world. But then there are times when if we don't decide what we're going to stand for, what we're going to believe, and how we're going to live, it becomes the difference between our existence as a Church in the earth and our non existence, our effectiveness as His body in the earth or our ineffectiveness. We're at that point in our world system and in the earth where the church must decide whether she's going to live by the world, or live by the Word.

The Church of Jesus Christ must decide whether or not she's going live in the natural or live in the supernatural realm through the blood of Jesus, by the power of the Holy Ghost. The Church of Jesus Christ must decide whether or not she's going to continue to live dependant on the world system or return to dependency on the system of the kingdom of God. The end is here, and the world we live in is testifying to that fact. Our world is reeling and rocking. Both in this nation and all over the world, both in our economic, political landscapes, and through disasters in the earth, seemingly caused by unusual weather patterns, the world we live in is testifying that the end is here. The last few years, we've seen deadly cyclones in Myanmar, deadly earthquakes in China and Japan, deadly hurricanes all over the southern and eastern coasts in the U.S. We've seen our stock market crash three or four times, hitting lows almost three times the low of the record low hit right before the Great Depression in 1929. We've seen our housing market collapse, our Car industry need a governmental bail-out to be sustained, while at the same time we've been at war with fundamentalist Islamic terrorists in Iraq, and Afghanistan sold out to the destruction of the systems of the western world.

Our world is on a downward spiral, fastly approaching the end of the age. The Gay marriage agenda in our nation is attempting to rewrite the moral code of the 10 commandments to redefine millenniums of human existence to fit this generation's unbridled lustful passions. The serpentine stranglehold of abortion continues to squeeze the life out of over 1.6 million wombs every year in our nation, wiping out nearly one-third of an entire generation born since 1973. The growing slave trade of pornography, homosexuality, human trafficking, and sexual perversion—not only accepted by the culture, but now shamelessly promoted by it—has claimed countless young men and women, pilfering the Kingdom of the Lord's inheritance. This is the context we find our world in as we approach the coming of the Lord. What's happening in our world? We are fast approaching the days of the generation of Lot. If God judged the generation of Lot, His word says He will necessarily need to judge this generation at the end of the age.

The Judgment on Sodom and Gomorrah

Gen 18:17 And the LORD said, Shall I hide from Abraham that thing which I do; 18 Seeing that Abraham shall surely become a great and mighty nation, and all the nations of the earth shall be blessed in him? 19 For I know him, that he will command his children and his household after him, and they shall keep the way of the LORD, to do

121

> *justice and judgment; that the LORD may bring upon Abraham that which he hath spoken of him. Gen 18:20 And the LORD said, Because the cry of Sodom and Gomorrah is great, and because their sin is very grievous; 21 I will go down now, and see whether they have done altogether according to the cry of it, which is come unto me; and if not, I will know.*

When God is determining the destiny of the Judgment of cities, He goes looking for a man He can share His anguish and pain for the situation of a people and a city. When He comes to Sodom to see the state of the city, He comes to the man Abraham and states; "Shall I hide from Abraham the thing which I do; Seeing that Abraham shall surely become a great and mighty nation...For I know him, that he will command his children and his household after him, and they shall keep the way of the Lord, to do justice and judgment;" He states 4 things that are vitally important to God placing upon His people His heart of anguish for intercession for the state of cities marked for Judgment.

1. He shall surely become a great and mighty nation
2. God knew him
3. He would command his children and his household after him, to keep the way of the Lord
4. They will do Justice and Judgment.

When God finds a man that will obey and follow him, not having to know everything or see everything before they obey him, and will teach his family to do the same, God will use that man to put His spirit of anguish and urgency in, to intercede for whole cities targeted for Judgment. God visited Abraham for the express purpose of getting His seed through Him for intercessory identification. In order for Abraham to know and intercede for the plans and purposes of God he had to experience what God would experience in sending His son to die for the sins of the world, know what God would feel about His son being offered up, and see with the eyes of God what God sees. God knew Abraham, that not only would he do this, but he would teach His children to do the same. So when God came to Abraham He came because, if there was one man that would intercede for the city, to make sure that God executed righteous Judgment on that city, it was Abraham. God wanted to spare the city, but there had to be enough people in the city who were not being held captive by the spirit of the city – *which was the Spirit of Leviathan*. However, there was only one family that would be spared the Judgment of that city, and even one from that family – Lots Wife- would not escape the Judgment being sent to that city, because she looked back and refused to come out of the city in her heart.

Come out from Among them

The only escape from the end-time Judgment on cities during the generation of Lot at the end of the age, is to completely obey the Lord, not based on seeing, but on faith, commanding your family to follow the Lord in the same manner, doing justice and judgment, and coming out of the sins of the city in your heart, not just in deed.

> *2Co 6:17 Wherefore come out from among them, and be ye separate, saith the Lord, and touch not the unclean thing; and I will receive you, 18 And will be a Father unto you, and ye shall be my sons and daughters, saith the Lord Almighty.*

It's not enough to come out in deed, but we must come out of the spirit of the world (Leviathan), in our hearts. In order to come out we must not just come out, we must separate ourselves, and not touch the unclean thing, to be received as a son/daughter of the Lord Almighty. The word "separate" is a Hebrew word "aphorize," which means to set boundaries. The word "touch" in speaking of not touching the unclean thing, is the Hebrew word "haptomai" which means; *to be set on fire.* When we set up boundaries then we can receive the fire of God that keeps the spirit of the world from you. You can't come out and stay out of the spirit of the world without setting boundaries. But once you set boundaries then God can baptize you in a fire that keeps the world at a noticeable distance from you. It was evident that Lot did not keep himself and His family from the spirit of the world. How do I know this? Firstly, his wife didn't make it. Secondly 2 Peter 2:7 says, he was vexed daily seeing and hearing the filthy conversation.

> *2Pe 2:7 And delivered just Lot, vexed with the filthy conversation of the wicked: 8 (For that righteous man dwelling among them, in seeing and hearing, vexed his righteous soul from day to day with their unlawful deeds;) 9 The Lord knows how to deliver the godly out of temptations, and to reserve the unjust unto the day of judgment to be punished: 10 But chiefly them that walk after the flesh in the lust of uncleanness, and despise government. Presumptuous are they, self-willed, they are not afraid to speak evil of dignities.*

God's Power to Deliver the Righteous from the Day of Judgment

Even when we allow ourselves to be vexed with the conversation of the wicked, seeing and hearing from day to day their unlawful deeds, God knows how to deliver the godly out of temptation and reserve the just from the Day of Judgment. God sends the angel of the Lord to Sodom and Gomorrah to separate the righteous – *Righteous Lot* – from the unrighteous – Sodom and Gomorrah -

because these twin cities had corrupted themselves. How did they corrupt themselves? Sodom and Gomorrah had been overtaken by the Spirit of Leviathan. Many people think that the sins of Sodom and Gomorrah were Homosexuality. However, this was not the sin that determined the fate of these sister cities. This sin was a part of a six-fold manifestation of the Spirit of Leviathan. These sins that determined the fate of Sodom are found in Ezekiel 16:48.

> *Eze 16:48 As I live, saith the Lord GOD, Sodom thy sister hath not done, she nor her daughters, as thou hast done, thou and thy daughters. 49 Behold, this was the iniquity of thy sister Sodom, **pride, fullness of bread**, and **abundance of idleness** was in her and in her daughters, **neither did she strengthen the hand of the poor and needy**. 50 And they were **haughty**, and **committed abomination before me**: therefore I took them away as I saw good.*

There were six sins that caused God to Judge Sodom and Gomorrah. These six things listed in Eze 16:48 are all rooted in the Spirit of Leviathan, or the Spirit of the world – *Lust of the Flesh, Lust of the Eye and the Pride of Life.*

1. Pride - Arrogance
2. Fullness of Bread - Worldliness
3. Abundance of Idleness – Pre-occupation with Pleasure
4. Refusing To Help the Poor & Needy – Selfish, Spoiled
5. Haughty - To think higher of self than others
6. Committed abomination - Sexual Sins of Homosexuality

Homosexuality was just a part of six sins that doomed the twin Cities of Sodom and Gomorrah. The source of Sodom and Gomorrah's sin was Leviathan - PRIDE.

125

The Cry of Sodom

I believe Genesis 18:20 is the most intriguing passage in the bible. God says that he was actually called to Sodom to the intercessor Abraham, not because Abraham's prayers called Him there, but the cry of Sodom called Him there. What was the cry of Sodom? Was it the righteous in Sodom praying about the sins of Sodom? I don't think so, because we see in Genesis 19 He could not find enough righteous from Abrahams intercession, to even spare the city. What was the cry of Sodom? I believe it was the actual region, the earth travailing from the sins of the region. How do I conclude this? *Rom 8:21,22 says, Because the creature itself also shall be delivered from the bondage of corruption into the glorious liberty of the children of God.; for we know that the whole creation groaneth and travaileth in pain together until now.*

The Greek word for *"Creature,"* or *"Creation"* is the word "ktisis" which means the original orderly formation of the created order. It's speaking of the earth in its original created order. What God was saying in Genesis 18 was that because of the corruption of sin of the children of God who was originally given the earth, the earth is crying out, moaning in pain because of the disorderly arrangement of the earth because of sin, corruption and immorality taking place in the earth. The earth cry's out to God when a region is being overtaken with corruption and immorality. Quite possibly, what Sodom's cry represented or looked like was disorder in the weather patterns, in the crops yielding fruit, and in the process of the seasons. It was the unnatural release of the earth's geographical process and order. Tornadoes, hurricanes, tsunami's, drought, famine, etc, is actually the earth's groan. When tragedy or abnormal catastrophes, and so-called natural disasters arise in the earth, it's either one of three things that are the root cause:

1. Man's Sin – Poverty, sickness, premature death, etc,
2. Satan's Rage – Man's inhumanity to Man
3. The Earth's Groan – Natural Disasters, and strange weather patterns.

Sodom's Cry was the disorderly arrangement of the earth's system because of the corruption and sin of the whole region. When the earth cry's out because of corruption and sin in the earth, God will always look for an intercessor to see if the region can be saved. In Genesis he gave Abraham a chance to intercede for Sodom before He judged the city.

Responsibilities of Intercessors over Cities

The first responsibility of intercessors in cities that are marked for judgment in a generation of degenerating morals and sin is to come out of those sins in their heart. This requires being set free from the Spirit of Leviathan through the 7 fold process seen in Chapters 4 and 5. The second responsibility of intercessors in cities that are marked for judgment are to establish Cities of Refuge for those that are also wanting to come out of the sins of the city in their heart. This entails establishing within the region networks of prayer, faith and obedience, (the Church) where people can go, to escape the impending judgment.

Escape to the Mountain

The key to where and what these places are can be seen in where the angel directed Lot and his family to go when he brought them out of the cities of Sodom and Gomorrah. The Angel of the Lord gave Lot and His family 4 directives that if they would follow, they would be spared the judgment of Sodom and Gomorrah.

> *Gen 19:15 And when the morning arose, then the angels hastened Lot, saying, Arise, take thy wife, and thy two daughters, which are here; lest thou be consumed in the iniquity of the city. 16 And while he lingered, the men laid hold upon his hand, and upon the hand of his wife, and upon the hand of his two daughters; the LORD being merciful unto him: and they brought him forth, and set him without the city. 17 And it came to pass, when they had brought them forth abroad, that he said, Escape for thy life; look not behind thee, neither stay thou in all the plain; escape to the mountain, lest thou be consumed.*

The Four things the angel of the Lord told Lot that are important for those that will build cities of refuge are;

1. Escape for thy Life
2. Look not behind thee
3. Neither stay in all the plain (place)
4. Escape to the Mountain

Escape for thy Life – Separate yourself from what vexes your Soul

To escape for your life refers, not only to your literal life, but to your inner, moral life, by separating from the sin or the corruption. The phrase *"look not behind you"* deals with your heart as well as leaving those things in a geographical proximity. It deals as much with our inner thoughts and hearts desires as it deal with looking at a place.

Look Not Behind Thee – Don't even think about it

To look back is to desire to hold on to those things and go back to them in your heart. The Angel could have said, "Let them go and don't even think about going after them anymore." It's not enough not to go after the things of the world; you've got to leave the very thoughts and desires for those things. Many Christians leave the acts of sin, as long as no one is watching them, but in their hearts they constantly think about those acts, talking about those days, and secretly desiring to go do those things again when no one is watching.

Don't Stay in the Same Place – Grow and Go from the Worlds Desires

The third command given to Lot and his family was, "Don't stay in the same place." You can't remain in the same place you were when you were in the world and grow and go from the things and desires of the world. You must go and grow closer to where God has commanded you to be and further from where you were. "Don't stay in the Place."

Escape to the Mountain – The Place of Prayer

And the last and most important command in relation to those that will build Cities of Refuge is "Escape to the Mountain." What does the mountain represent?

> *Isa 2:2 And it shall come to pass in the last days, that the mountain of the LORD'S house shall be established in the top of the mountains, and shall be exalted above the hills; and all nations shall flow unto it. 3 And many people shall go and say, Come ye, and let us go up to the mountain of the LORD,*

to the house of the God of Jacob; and he will teach us of his ways, and we will walk in his paths: for out of Zion shall go forth the law, and the word of the LORD from Jerusalem.

Isa 56:7 Even them will I bring to my holy mountain, and make them joyful in my house of prayer: their burnt offerings and their sacrifices shall be accepted upon mine altar; for mine house shall be called an house of prayer for all people.

The mountains in scripture represent kingdoms. And in this instance we can see from the scriptures above that the mountains represent the House of God, and specifically the House of Prayer. If we are going to be spared the shaking and Judgment of cities at the end of the age we're going to have to be restored to our identity and place of prayer in the body of Christ.

Holiness – The Call of Our Cities

God wants Houses of Prayer to pray for God's purposes for Cities. These prayers are going to be what spares whole cities from Judgment. After God revealed to me the meaning of the spirit of Leviathan, and how this spirit is holding whole cities in its grips and tentacles, God began dealing with me about Holy Cities, and how cities can overcome this spirit of Leviathan and the judgment of cities at the end of the age.

*Rev 21:10 And he carried me away in the spirit to a great and high mountain, and shewed me that **great city, the holy Jerusalem**, descending out of heaven from God.*

In Revelation 21:2 John says, "I John, saw the holy city, New Jerusalem, coming down from God out of heaven as a bride adorned for husband.....*having the glory of God: and her light was like unto a stone most precious, even like a jasper stone, clear as crystal."* I believe that it is the purpose of the people of God to be builders of Cities, not churches. The building of the Church is the function of Christ, the Head. Jesus said, *"Upon this Rock I will build My Church."* The function of the church, his people in the earth, is to build cities, filling them with the glory of God, and the principles of the kingdom of God, making them Holy, and New. (Matt 16:19) *"Whatsoever ye bind/loose on earth/heaven will be bound/loosed in Heaven/earth.*) Jesus does not make anything or anyone holy, that's the job of those that come into contact and intimacy with a Holy God. He says; *be ye Holy, as I am Holy.* It's our command to be Holy, and it's our responsibility to make our cities Holy. This holiness is not just talking about morality and sin issues, but it speaks of the callings and purposes of people and cities. Holiness deals with distinctiveness and uniqueness of persons, their call and their purpose. God is holy because there's none like him. He's unique; He's distinct, other than, completely separate from any other.

What is Holiness

Holiness deals with fulfilling your distinct purpose and walking in your distinct calling in the earth. Each individual has a unique purpose and calling that no one else has, and each city has a unique purpose and calling that no one else has or can fulfill. The New Jerusalem being a Holy City speaks directly to its purpose being restored and it's calling being fulfilled. What is the purpose and calling of Jerusalem? The word *"Jerusalem"* is a word that in the Hebrew means; *founded on peace, or the city of peace.* SO THE PURPOSE OF JERUSALEM IS TO BE A CITY OF PEACE. THE CALLING OF JERUSALEM IS TO BRING PEACE TO THE WORLD.

131

Presently in 2013 everyone knows that Jerusalem in not a city of peace. It is the most tumultuous, divisive, dangerously violent city in the earth. It's full of strife, bitterness, hatred, division, wars and threats and rumors of war, as the two brothers from Abraham - *Isaac and Ishmael* - fight over the promise land. It is because the spirit of Leviathan has intertwined with that city's destiny and calling, and has influenced rulers and leaders for centuries and millenniums with its flattery, deceit, and its corrupt commerce. However, the vision that John saw in the revelation was a vision of a New Jerusalem, a Holy City, and a city, whose walls were rebuilt. Rebuilt walls means that the fighting, strife, and division had ceased and the threat of war had been erased. In scripture walls around a city were deterrents for war, for intruders, invaders, for enemies. A city without walls was a place open to enemy invasion and a place where anything and everything goes.

Pro 25:28 *He that hath no rule over his own spirit is like a city that is broken down, and without walls.*

What walls were rebuilt in the city of Jerusalem making it a Holy, new City? They were the walls of Intercession. Isaiah 62:6 says *I have set watchmen on your walls, O Jerusalem; they shall never hold their peace day or night...till He makes Jerusalem a praise in the earth.* Intercession for the city of Jerusalem to become a Holy City, and a praise in the earth, is one of the vital attributes of the walls of the city being rebuilt, and at the return of Heaven to earth at the end of Human History, it is what enabled this city to be seen as a New City, a Holy City, a City founded on its purpose of peace and oneness of spirit, soul and body.

This is what is referred to when God speaks of a Holy City; its' referring to that city or persons in that city fulfilling the distinct purpose and calling for that city or nation, or for their life. For a city to be made new what's holding that city from its purpose must be removed. God told me it's the spirit of Leviathan that is holding my city and the cities of the earth from its purposes. Until we focus on rebuilding the walls of our cities, we will not see the Glory of God. I believe the new thing that God is doing in the earth is that he's transitioning His church from being builders of churches to being builders of Cities, filling them with the glory of God. If the new thing is the Church building cities and filling them with the Glory of God, as opposed to building buildings and filling them with people, until we get our minds off of coming to church **to see** the glory of God and get it on leaving the church **to be** the glory of God we will not see our Cities changed by the power of God. Until we get free from the spirit of Leviathan we will never truly see the glory of God in our lives or our cities.

The Expression of Leviathan in our Cities and Churches in the End-Times

The Hebrew word for Leviathan is livya^tha^n, or liv-yaw-thawn' and it means; a wreathed animal, that is, a serpent (especially the crocodile or some other large sea monster); figuratively the constellation of the dragon; also as a symbol of Babylon: - leviathan, mourning. This Hebrew word has an even further meaning. The Hebrew word for Leviathan – livya^tha^n - comes from the root Hebrew word - la^va^h law-vaw' – which is the primitive root of Leviathan; and properly it means to *twine, that is, (by implication) to unite, to remain; also to borrow (as a form of obligation) or (causatively) to lend: - abide with, borrow (-er), cleave, join (self), lend (-er).*

This spirit of Leviathan in the church intertwines with the things of the Spirit of God in the church. It is the serpent spirit of Babylon, an economic, financial and political spirit operating in the church destroying, burning up and blaspheming the name of God. (Psa. 74:1-8)

Psa 74:1 O God, why hast thou cast us off forever? Why doth thine anger smoke against the sheep of thy pasture? 2 Remember thy congregation, which thou hast purchased of old; the rod of thine inheritance, which thou hast redeemed; this mount Zion, wherein thou hast dwelt.

3 Lift up thy feet unto the perpetual desolations; even all that the enemy hath done wickedly in the sanctuary. ___4 Thine enemies roar in the midst of thy congregations; they set up their ensigns for signs.___

5 A man was famous according as he had lifted up axes upon the thick trees. 6 But now they break down the carved work thereof at once with axes and hammers. 7 They have cast fire into thy sanctuary, they have defiled by casting down the dwelling place of thy name to the ground. 8 They said in their hearts, Let us destroy them together: they have burned up all the synagogues of God in the land. 9 We see not our signs: there is no more any prophet: neither is there among us any that knoweth how long. 10 O God, how long shall the adversary reproach? shall the enemy blaspheme thy name forever?

The fall of Babylon is the breaking of the spirit of Leviathan in the church so the church refuses the system and spirit of the world and the mark of the beast. Rev. 14:8

7 saying with a loud voice, Fear God, and give glory to him; for the hour of his judgment is come: and worship him that made heaven, and earth, and the sea, and the fountains of waters.

8 and there followed another angel, saying, Babylon is fallen, is fallen, that great city, because she made all nations drink of the wine of the wrath of her fornication.

9 And the third angel followed them, saying with a loud voice, If any man worship the beast and his image, and receive his mark in his forehead, or in his hand,

10 The same shall drink of the wine of the wrath of God, which is poured out without mixture into the cup of his indignation; and he shall be tormented with fire and brimstone in the presence of the holy angels, and in the presence of the Lamb:

Babylon the great, the spirit of Leviathan is the mother of harlots and abominations of the earth

Rev 17:3 So he carried me away in the spirit into the wilderness: and I saw a woman sit upon a scarlet coloured beast, full of names of blasphemy, having seven heads and ten horns.

4. and the woman was arrayed in purple and scarlet colour, and decked with gold and precious stones and pearls, having a golden cup in her hand full of abominations and filthiness of her fornication:

5. and upon her forehead was a name written, MYSTERY, BABYLON THE GREAT, THE MOTHER OF HARLOTS AND ABOMINATIONS OF THE EARTH.

The church must have the spirit of Leviathan broken off of her to come out of the world Babylonian system before it falls and we partake of her sins.

> *Rev 18:1 and after these things I saw another angel come down from heaven, having great power; and the earth was lightened with his glory.*

> *2 And he cried mightily with a strong voice, saying, Babylon the great is fallen, is fallen, and is become the habitation of devils, and the hold of every foul spirit, and a cage of every unclean and hateful bird.*

> *3 For all nations have drunk of the wine of the wrath of her fornication, and the kings of the earth have committed fornication with her, and the merchants of the earth are waxed rich through the abundance of her delicacies. 4 And I heard another voice from heaven, saying,* **Come out of her, my people, that ye be not partakers of her sins, and that ye receive not of her plagues.**

Babylon the great is the system of the world with its merchants and lust attempting to make profit and make an end to all.

> *9 And the kings of the earth, who have committed fornication and lived deliciously with her, shall bewail her, and lament for her, when they shall see the smoke of her burning,*

> *10 Standing afar off for the fear of her torment, saying, Alas, alas, that great city Babylon, that mighty city! for in one hour is thy judgment come.*

11 And the merchants of the earth shall weep and mourn over her; for no man buyeth their merchandise any more:

12 The merchandise of gold, and silver, and precious stones, and of pearls, and fine linen, and purple, and silk, and scarlet, and all thyine wood, and all manner vessels of ivory, and all manner vessels of most precious wood, and of brass, and iron, and marble, 15. the merchants of these things, which were made rich by her, shall stand afar off for the fear of her torment, weeping and wailing,

16. And saying, **_Alas, alas, that great city, that was clothed in fine linen, and purple, and scarlet, and decked with gold, and precious stones, and pearls!_**

17. For in one hour so great riches is come to naught. And every shipmaster, and all the company in ships, and sailors, and as many as trade by sea, stood afar off,

CHAPTER 8

BUILDING CITIES OF REFUGE

*9 The LORD also will be a refuge for the oppressed,
a refuge in times of trouble. 10 And they that know
thy name will put their trust in thee: for thou,
LORD, hast not forsaken them that seek thee. 11
Sing praises to the LORD, which dwelleth in Zion:
declare among the people his doings. Psalms 9:9-11*

As the church is positioned for the coming Great and terrible day of the Lord our calling in establishing Holy Cities where God's glory is being poured out and His presence dwells is going to become increasingly vital. As the Judgment is released on the Babylonian world system, those that have come out of Babylon and have made Jesus their refuge will have protection, provision and blessing.

The Cities of Refuge in scripture were towns in the Kingdom of Israel and Kingdom of Judah in which the perpetrators of manslaughter could claim the right of asylum; outside of these cities, blood vengeance against such perpetrators was allowed by law.[1] The Torah names just six cities as being cities of refuge: Golan, Ramoth, and Bosor, on the east of the Jordan River, and Kedesh, Shechem, and Hebron on the western side.

Cities of Refuge or Sanctuaries

Cities of Refuge are symbols of God's unconditional love and constant presence among people. The most significant aspect of a City of Refuge was that it was, in every meaning of the word, a sanctuary. A sanctuary is, of course, a place of protection. But a sanctuary is also a temple to God--designed and built according to God's instructions and cared for by priests. Therefore when we refer to building cities of Refuge, we're actually referring to building the city house of prayer in a City, where God's glory and presence rests and dwells,

Build Me a Sanctuary

In the Old testament God instructed Moses to build a symbol of His presence among the Israelites: *"And build for Me a sanctuary so that I may dwell among them"* (Exodus 25:8). We learn from scripture that the sanctuary was not meant as a house for God. God had *not* said, "And build for Me a sanctuary so that I may dwell in it," but, *"And build Me a sanctuary so that I may dwell among them."* At the very end of the Book of Numbers, we are again reminded what a sanctuary is.

A sanctuary--be it a temple of marble and gold or a City of Refuge to which criminals flee--is a powerful, concrete symbol of God's constant presence among people. God dwells with people, whoever they are, whatever they have done. His covenant with them is unshakable: His love is unconditional. No matter who you are and what you have done, God does not abandon you. God recognizes that people make mistakes. He always gives us another chance. And this is what the hapless offender--ridden with guilt and remorse-was to learn in the City of Refuge.

These *Cities of Refuge* form one of the Old Testament pictures of the sinner, and of the coming gospel of salvation. God often used such *pictures* to teach the Jewish people great gospel truths. Just as we know that youthful readers like a story-book all the better when it has pictures in it; so God taught the early church, when it was in a state of *"childhood,"* by means of similar *pictures* or *types;* and this present picture was one of them. It represented, and still represents, the sinner who has broken the Divine law as pursued by an avenger, JUSTICE, following with drawn sword, exclaiming, *"The soul that sins—it must surely die!"* (Ezekiel 18:4) *"Be assured that the wicked will not go unpunished!"* (Proverbs 11:21) In the New Testament we know that Jesus took on His body on a tree, our sins, and became a refuge for our soul.

In addition to this is being a picture applying to the individual souls of men, it is also a picture of a glorious CITY and regions of the earth at the end of the age, *"salvation being its walls, bulwarks,"* and it's open gates. The sinner is exhorted to "escape there;" to "linger not in all the plain;" to "flee for his life, lest he be consumed!" (Genesis 19:17) That city is a place where the Lordship of *Jesus becomes* the sinner's Refuge and Jesus the sinner's Friend. Once within its walls, no enemy can touch him— no sword can terrify him. He can triumphantly exclaim, "Who shall separate me from the love of Christ!" (Romans 8:35)

The Coming Day of the Lord

At the end of the age God is raising up His Church in the context of day and night prayer meetings in the nations of the earth to prepare the Church to build these Cities of Refuge for the coming day of the Lord. God is using many in this context of day and night prayer to bring revelation and sound the alarm concerning the coming of the unique dynamics of the day of the Lord.

What is this Day of the Lord? Not too many believers in Christendom have an adequate understanding of what the Day of the Lord is. Many in the body of Christ are unaware of the unique dynamics of this day and what our actual preparation for this day entails. The day of the Lord is most talked about in the book of Zephaniah, Malachi, Joel, and the Revelation of Jesus Christ. However Peter, in quoting the book of Joel describes this day in correlation with the spirit of God that will be poured out on all flesh in the last days in Acts 2:20, saying, *"The sun will be turned*

141

to darkness and the moon to blood before the coming of the Great and Terrible day of the Lord."

There are two main characteristics of this day of the Lord. It will be a Great day, but it will also be a terrible day.

GREAT DAY - The Day of the Lord will have "great" attributes and characteristics for those that respond to Him as He releases the greatest manifestation of His power in natural human history. He is going to change the understanding and expression of Christianity in the whole earth in one generation. It will be the greatest time for the church in history.

VERY TERRIBLE DAY - The day of the Lord will also be the most severe time of God's judgment ever on earth since the beginning of human history. (Rev. 6-20)

> *...Yet once more I shake not only the earth, but heaven also...that the things, which cannot be shaken, remain. (Heb 12, 26-27) The four angels, who had been prepared for the house and day....were released to kill a third of mankind. (Rev. 9:15-16)*

There has never been a day like this before on the face of the earth. Not in power or pressure. Not the cloud and pillar of fire of Moses in the wilderness. Not World War II, where 50 million died, not Hitler, Stalin, not even the Pentecostal Revivals of Azusa or the Day of Pentecost.

> *I will pour My Spirit out on all flesh.... I will show wonders in the heavens and in the earth: Blood, fire and pillars of smoke.....(Joel 2:28-30)*

> *For there will be great tribulation, such has not been since the beginning of the world until this time, no, nor ever shall be. (Matt 24.21)*

The great and terrible dimensions of the Day of the Lord will both increase dramatically the closer we get to the return of Jesus and will find their fullest expressions in the final 3 ½ years of natural human history. I believe we are in the warning years, birth pangs for the church to receive an urgency and fervency to get in the prayer position to be PRE-PRAYER-ED (prayed up) for this day. I believe in 2012 God began positioning in his end-time Church, Josephs, Daniels and many end-time forerunners to rise up and begin to declare and pre-prayer with wisdom, revelation (dreams & visions) and wealth, for the preservation of His people during the coming of the Great and Terrible day of the Lord.

In this visitation on the date 11-11-11 in Detroit Michigan at *THE CALL DETROIT*, the Spirit of God spoke to me and told me that the Day of Lord is fast approaching, and that 11-11-11 signals a pivotal time of coming together in the church across racial and socio-economic divides to begin seeking the face of My Son for the release of divine *Love, Peace, Reconciliation, Protection and Provision* towards preparation for the coming of this day. He further said that the church of this generation is not ready for the unique dynamics of this day. He said that this day will cause offense and a falling away of many that name the name of Christ if they are not adequately prepared in prayer. He said if my people don't clearly understand this coming day and adequately PRE-PRAYER for it, my church will not be able to endure and stand in this day.

> *Blow the trumpet in Zion, sanctify a fast, call a solemn assembly: Gather the people, sanctify the congregation, assemble the elders, gather the children, and those that suck the breasts: let the bridegroom go*

forth of his chamber, and the bride out of her closet. Let the priests, the ministers of the LORD, weep between the porch and the altar, and let them say, Spare thy people, O LORD (Joel 2:15-17).

Sacred Assemblies Coming to the Church

Sacred Assemblies like the 24hr Call Detroit are God's prescribed method to either avert the judgment completely, or lessen it in a geographical region, or prepare a generation to stand without offense in the midst of the economic, environmental, and military crisis that are clearly seen in Joel and passages that clearly articulate the conditions of the end of the age. Prayer meetings are God's remedy of response to impending judgment. I believe this Detroit Call to 24 hours of prayer, as well as many of the other prayer meetings on this date in that year was given, not to be a one-time event, but as a prescription of what we will do during the time of the *Day of the Lord*. God's remedy for preservation, protection and provision for his people during this coming day, is night and day prayer meetings in the nations of the earth.

Refuge in the Times of Trouble

In establishing and building cities of refuge at the end of the age, the protection is not necessarily in your geographical proximity or place but in your relational proximity with a person in that region. When God inhabits cities He's going to come to those regions to establish a habitation with the people of that region out of their seeking His face. It's a person that's going to be our refuge, not a place. Psalm 46:1 says **God is our refuge and strength** a very present help in the time of trouble. Psalm 9 gives the scriptural blueprint for making God our refuge.

> *Psa 9:9 The LORD also will be a refuge for the oppressed, a refuge in times of trouble. 10 And they that know thy name will put their trust in thee: for thou, LORD, hast not forsaken them that seek thee. 11 Sing praises to the LORD, which dwelleth in Zion: declare among the people his doings.*

There are 4 steps to establishing cities of refuge from these verses.

1. **Intimacy:** When times of trouble come it's those that <u>know His name that will put their trust in Him</u> (Psa. 9:10). The Hebrew word for the English word *"know"* is the word "yada," which means to know <u>*intimately*</u> as to produce fruit, as in *Genesis 4:1 Adam knew Eve and she conceived.*

2. **Seek Him:** Those that are intimately related with the Lord when trouble comes will seek Him in prayer and fasting out of that relational intimacy.

3. **Sing Praises to the Lord:** After the prayer of seeking the Lord, the end-time church will build cities of refuge in the times of trouble by Singing praises to the Lord. Worship and Praise will be a vital part of the end-time prayer movement that is protected during the times of Judgment of cities

4. **Declare His doings among the people:** Sharing and testifying about the Goodness, provision and protection of the Lord will be another main weapon and tool for building cities of refuge in the time of Judgment of Cities. Revelation 12:11 says, the saints will overcome Satan in the unique dynamics at the end of the age by the Blood of the Lamb – Jesus, and by the Word of their testimony – the Word of God, and testifying about the goodness of God

145

CHAPTER 9

THE FOUR STEPS TO BUILDING CITIES OF REFUGE

Psa 9:9 The LORD also will be a refuge for the oppressed, a refuge in times of trouble. 10 And they that know thy name will put their trust in thee: for thou, LORD, hast not forsaken them that seek thee. 11 Sing praises to the LORD, which dwelleth in Zion: declare among the people his doings.

Step #1: Intimacy and The Bridal Paradigm

The first step in building cities of Refuge from Psalm 9:9-11 is knowing the name of the Lord, so as to put our trust in Him. This is better known as developing an intimate relationship with the Lord that produces fruit, as when a bridegroom and his bride come together in intimacy to produce offspring. At the end of the age, before Jesus returns, the Spirit of God is going to restore our bridal identity back to the body of Christ, taking us to a place of intimacy with our bridegroom God, which causes us to *trust Him* and *seek Him* with all our hearts to come to us in our times of trouble.

> *Rev 22:17 and the Spirit and the bride say, Come. And let him that hears say, Come*

We will hear much about the ***Bridal paradigm*** as we approach the coming of the Lord and the Kingdom of God. The word paradigm means perspective or view. Thus, we refer to the "bridal perspective or view" of the kingdom of God. We see the Kingdom through the eyes of a wholehearted Bride with loyal devoted love. If we do not feel loved and in love, then we more easily compromise, lack courage and become spiritually bored. The Holy Spirit for the first time in history will universally emphasize

146

the Church's spiritual identity as Jesus' Bride. This scripture does not prophesy the Spirit and the family say "Come." Nor does it say the Spirit and the army say come, nor the Spirit and the kingdom say come, nor the body, nor the temple, neither does it say the Spirit and the priesthood say come, but only *the Spirit and the Bride.* Forever, we rejoice in the reality of our spiritual identity as God's army, family, body, temple, priesthood and kingdom, but at the end of the age the last and main identity he will emphasis and restore is our spiritual identity as His Bride.

The Bridegroom Message Is a Call to Active Intimacy with God

The Spirit searches all things, yes, the deep things of God...12 we have received...the Spirit...that we might know (experience) the things that have been freely given to us by God. (1 Cor. 2:10-12)

God's invitation is for us to experience the deep things of His heart (emotions, desire, affection and thoughts about us). Thus, to enjoy *active intimacy* with Jesus that includes understanding and feeling His heart. Thus, the Bridal message is experiencing Jesus' emotions (desire, affections) for us. We must return to our bridal identity in the body of Christ as the Bride of Christ. As women are the sons of God, so men are the Bride of Christ, both describe our position of privilege before God, rather than pointing to something that is intrinsically male or female. Most Christian women do not struggle with the idea of being sons of God because they do not see it as a call to be less feminine. However, often, men struggle with being the Bride of Christ because they wrongly conclude that it is a call to become less masculine, because they do not understand it as a position of privilege that enables us to encounter His heart. Some of the greatest men of God functioned in the essential reality of the bridal identity.

147

King David was Israel's greatest warrior king, yet he was a lovesick worshipper, ravished by God's desire for him and fascinated by His beauty (Ps. 27:4). One of the central issues of David's life, as a man after God's own heart, was in being a student of God's emotions and affections. John the apostle was called the Son of Thunder and he described himself five times as the one whom Jesus loved (Jn. 13:23; 19:26; 20:2; 21:7, 20).

John the Baptist was the fiery prophet that Jesus called the "greatest man" (Mt. 11:11). He understood Jesus as the Bridegroom God (Jn. 3:29). In other words, experiencing the reality of being the Bride of Christ does not undermine one's masculinity, but rather it strengthens and establishes it. To understand Jesus as a passionate Bridegroom is to soon see ourselves as cherished Bride. Intimacy causes our hearts to be lovesick for Jesus (inflamed; enraptured; overcome by His love).

> *O daughters of Jerusalem, if you find my Beloved (Jesus)...tell Him I am lovesick! (Song 5:8)*

What Is The Bridegroom Message? (Mt. 22:2; 25:1)

Jesus the Bridegroom is filled with tender mercy – He is gentle with our weakness. We often confuse rebellion and immaturity. God is angry at rebellion, but He has a heart of tenderness towards sincere believers that seek to obey Him. He enjoys us even in our weakness.

> *He delivered me because He delighted in me. 35 Your gentleness made me great. (Ps. 18:19, 35) If You, LORD, should mark iniquities...who could stand? 4 But there is forgiveness with You, that You may be feared. (Ps. 130:3-4)*

148

Jesus the Bridegroom has a heart of gladness (happy heart) – Jesus had more gladness than any man in history (Heb. 1:9). Most of Church history has viewed God as mostly mad or mostly sad when He relates to us. However, Jesus is mostly glad when He relates to us, even in our weakness.

> *God has anointed you with the oil of gladness more than your companions. (Heb. 1:9)*

Jesus the Bridegroom has fiery affections – He has burning desire and longing.

> *As the Father loved Me, I also have loved you; abide in my love. (Jn. 15:9)*

Jesus the Bridegroom is zealous – He destroys all that hinders love and injures His Church (Zech.1:14; 8:2; Ezek. 38:18-19; Rev. 19:2; Prov. 6:34)

> *Jealousy is a husband's fury, therefore, He will not spare in the day of vengeance. (Prov. 6:34)*

Jesus the Bridegroom possesses indescribable beauty – He fascinates our hearts (Ps. 27:4).

> *One thing I have desired of the LORD...that I may dwell in the house of the LORD all the days of my life, to behold the beauty of the LORD... (Ps. 27:4)*

> *Your eyes will see the King in His beauty.... (Isa. 33:17)*

Encounters with a lovesick God will energize the Church with a spirit of prayer with courage. We cry, "Come", both upwardly to Jesus and outwardly to people (evangelism, discipleship) differently with the Bridal paradigm. The Church will be cleansed by experiencing the cherishing heart of Jesus.

> *That He might...cleanse her...by the Word...27 present her...a glorious church...29 for no one ever hated his flesh, but nourishes and cherishes it, as the Lord does the Church. (Eph. 5:26-29)*

The 3-Fold Intercessory Cry for Jesus to Come

1. *Come NEAR US in intimacy* (individual breakthrough of my heart in God)

2. *Come TO US in revival* (regional or national breakthrough of the Spirit in revival)

3. *Come FOR US in the sky* (historical breakthrough by the Second Coming of Jesus).

The 2-fold expression of the Bride's cry for Jesus to come

1. *Worship* — "We love you, we worship you, we beckon you to come by our love."

2. *Intercession* — "We need you, we pray for you to come and release revival power.

It's a two-dimensional cry upward to God and outward to people. It's *Vertical* — an upward call to Jesus to come to us in breakthrough power (near us/to us/for us). *It's Horizontal* — an outward call to people to come to Jesus as the Bridegroom King. We call believers *(revival, discipleship)* and unbelievers *(evangelism)* to experience the Bridegroom God. Most of the

Western Church today is out of sync with this purpose of God. Many things will change. What will help bring about this change? The Holy Spirit is raising up forerunners.

Forerunners are those who are one short step ahead of others in walking out and announcing what the Holy Spirit will soon emphasize universally. The Spirit anoints what He emphasizes. Jesus will only come (near us/to us/for us) in response to a praying Church, and not in a vacuum. He only comes by invitation of His covenant people. In the Father's sovereignty, He has decreed to work only in partnership with a praying Church. Ministry programs can be helpful, but must not exist at the expense of the prayer ministry, which is the primary mandate of the Church. It is important to know where we are going and how to get there. The End-Time Church will surely be victorious as we are anointed in intercession in our bridal identity.

> *"...that He might sanctify and cleanse her...by the Word, that He might present...a Glorious Church...that she should be holy..." (Eph. 5:26-27)*
> *"A great multitude...of all nations...and tongues...before the Lamb" (Rev. 7:9)*

> *"Let us be glad...for the marriage of the Lamb has come, His wife has made herself READY....arrayed in fine linen, clean and bright..." (Rev. 19: 7-8)*

Step #2: Seek His Face

The next step in building cities of Refuge from Psalm 9:10-11 are seeking His face....*for thou, LORD, hast not forsaken them that seek thee (v 10).* II Chronicles 7:14 is our prescription for how to turn or lessen the Judgment of God in a region in the earth.

II Chronicles 7:14 says, "If my people which are called by my name will humble themselves and pray and seek my face and turn from their wicked ways, then will I hear from heaven and will forgive their sins and heal their land.

This verse in 2nd Chronicles makes it clear that the answer to the problems of this nation or world is not the world. The answer is not in the church preaching to the world to turn from their sins, but in the church, the body of believers in Christ being compelled to turn from their own wicked, sinful and religious ways. This verse is God speaking to his people saying, during times of drought, disaster and impending destruction; *IF MY PEOPLE* would humble themselves, pray and seek my face and turn from their wicked ways I would hear from heaven, forgive their sins and heal their land. For a land to be healed, God's people must first repent. We must start with the sins of our hearts before we can go on to the sins of the world. However, what he challenges His people to repent of is what's most interesting. What do God's people in the church need to repent of? Is it sexual sins? Is it drunkenness? What is it that the church needs to repent for? Is it idolatry? Is it covetousness? We definitely need to repent of all of that in the modern Church, but this is not what God is speaking of when he tells them to turn from their wicked ways.

What are the Church's Wicked Ways - Leviathan

II Chronicles 7:14 declares that we are to turn from our wicked ways. But what are the wicked ways He's referring to? The wicked ways of His people are the reason that the Lord shuts up heaven that there's no blessing, but cursing, no healing but sickness. But what are the wicked ways of His people? What God calls wicked is far from what we think of when we think of wickedness. When we think of wickedness we think of sexual immorality, debauchery, licentiousness and all types of lasciviousness. However, when God tells us to turn from our wickedness he's not just speaking of immoral lifestyle habits, as much as he is speaking of our backsliding from our spiritual disciplines in seeking His face. He's speaking of the breaking of the covenants man made with God to give Him access into the earth He gave us. God's people are the ones who give God access into the earth, because the earth has been given to the children of men (Psalm 115:16). When we stop looking to Him, inviting Him into our situations in the earth, we cause the earth to be absent of its' source of blessing, healing, and prosperity. God calls wicked, a people that call themselves by the name of God but have allowed the spirit of Leviathan to cause us to become prideful, acting and living as if we can do what God has called us to do and be what God has called us to be in the earth without God, without prayer. God, in 2nd Chronicles 7:14 calls wickedness a people that call themselves by the name of God, but do not pray. He calls wickedness a people that are called by the name of God but will not seek His face. His remedy for a land that needs healing is for His people to turn from their wicked ways and REPENT of their PRIDE, PRAYERLESSNESS, and UNWILLINGNESS TO SEEK HIS FACE.

The land was created by God, for man, to be inhabited by God through His relationship with man, whom He made His landlord in the earth. When Adam sinned and locked God out, the earth became filled with sin, rebellion, sickness, disease, Satan and his demons. In order for God to regain access back into the earth again he had to find another man to cut covenant with. Through Abraham God found a man and a people to cut covenant with to get His son into the earth to begin the healing and restoration process of the earth and man. Prayer is that access and key for God's reentry into the earth to heal our land. As Adam's pride locked God out of the earth, Jesus' humility gave God access back into the earth

Luk 3:21 Now when all the people were baptized, it came to pass, that Jesus also being baptized, and praying, the heaven was opened, 22 And the Holy Ghost descended in a bodily shape like a dove upon him, and a voice came from heaven, which said, Thou art my beloved Son; in thee I am well pleased.

Humility and submission to God's will and plan for our lives, families and destinies in the earth are always the key to an open heaven and God's access into the earth. Pride always closes the windows of heaven and shuts God out. Pride is the epitome of man's wickedness. It is the sin of all sins; it is the sin that caused Satan's demise in Ezekiel 28:14

You were anointed as a guardian cherub, for so I ordained you. You were on the holy mount of God; you walked among the fiery stones. You were blameless in your ways from the day you were created till wickedness was found in you. Through your widespread trade you were filled with violence, and you sinned. So I drove you in disgrace from the mount of God, and I expelled you, O guardian cherub, from among the fiery stones. YOUR HEART BECAME PROUD ON ACCOUNT OF YOUR BEAUTY. Ezek. 28:14(NIV)

It was this same sin of pride that caused Adam & Eve to be put out of the Garden of Eden. As a matter of fact this account in Ezekiel 28 sounds eerily like what happened to our first parents. Adam and Eve, through the sin of pride, were put out of the Garden of Eden, having turned over the title deed of the earth to Satan. They succumbed to the prideful proposition of Satan, to do what God told them to do - *have dominion over all the earth that God created and gave to them* - without God, without having to seek God, without having to wait on God, or look to God. This is the definition of the sin of Pride. This is the sin that began the release into the earth of all the wickedness, depravity, and corruption that is in the earth now- the sin of pride.

The destiny of a people that are called by the name of God, praying and seeking the face of God is a healed, whole, God-centered land that is once again fruitful and prosperous. The remedy for a sick land is a people that turn from Leviathan, their pride and prayerlessness and began once again to seek the face of God. The Church that has failed to fulfill her purpose in the earth as a House of Prayer has allowed into the earth Satan, and the curse of sin, sickness and disease that has caused the earth to be a barren wilderness in need of healing. *Mark 11:17 says, "My House shall be called of all nations a house of prayer, but you have (allowed it) to become a den of thieves."* When the Church fails to fulfill her purpose as a house of prayer we make the atmosphere conducive for Satan, the thief that comes to kill, steal and destroy, to exist and have his way in our midst. We must wake up and repent of our pride, turning from our wickedness, back to our true purpose and mission in the earth, to become a house of prayer.

Step #3: Sing Praises To The Lord

The next step in building cities of Refuge from Psalm 9:9-11 are found in singing praises to the Lord…. *Sing praises to the LORD, which dwells in Zion* (v.11). God's government flows from prophetic worship based on the beauty of holiness. God is restoring the spiritual weapons of worship with intercession in prophetic worship. The End of the Age government and power is linked to singers and musicians. The Davidic Church is one that functions as a house of prayer. It is remarkable how central singers are to the End of the Age drama. Corporate intercessory worship is the *primary means* God has chosen to release His government (power). It is the highest expression of His government in time and eternity and is the most powerful weapon that exists. It is the front line of defense in our war against darkness. The New Testament Church sowed the seed of God's order of worship as first established on earth in David's Tabernacle using psalms, hymns, and spiritual songs (Eph 5:18-19; Col. 3:16; Jas. 5:13).

> *14 Simon (Peter) declared how God...visited the Gentiles to take out of them a people for His name. 15 With this the words of the prophets agree, as it is written: 16 "After this I will return and will rebuild the Tabernacle of David, which has fallen down; I will rebuild its ruins, and I will set it up; 17 so that the rest of mankind may seek the LORD..." (Acts 15:14-17)*

Church history parallels Israel's history. Whenever God released a season of revival to restore what was lost, we see the aspects of David's order of worship released in that generation. Every revival in history has received an aspect of God's "new song and music" for that generation.

In the end-time revival at the end of the age, there will be another great worship movement that will call the Son to the earth at the time of the Second Coming. In the millennium, the Millennial worship movement will call the Father to the earth (Rev. 21:3). The End-Time prayer and worship movement will be mature and operate in great authority in prayer and worship. (Rev. 5:8; 6:9-11; 8:3-5). The "bowls of prayer" will be full in heaven before Jesus releases the seven seals of judgment on the earth.

> *8 When He had taken the scroll, the four living creatures and the twenty-four elders fell down before the Lamb, each having a harp, and golden bowls full of incense, which are the prayers of the saints. 9 And they sang a new song, saying: "You*

are worthy to take the scroll, and to open its seals;
for You were slain, and have redeemed us to God
by Your blood... (Rev. 5:8-9)

The new song originates at God's Throne and is dynamically related to Jesus' Coming to earth (Ps. 33:3-14; 40:3-10; 96:1; 98:1; 149:1-9; Rev. 5:8-4; 14:2-3). God promised to establish intercessors who will never be silent until He restores Jerusalem.

6 I have set watchmen on your walls...they shall
never hold their peace (be silent, NAS) day or
night...7 give Him no rest till He
establishes...Jerusalem a praise in the earth. (Isa.
62:6-7)

Isa. 42:10-13 with Rev. 22:17 gives us the clearest picture of the End-Time Church "praying in conjunction with prophetic singing" to invite the Second Coming of Jesus. The prophetic "new song" will be released in all nations leading to Jesus' Second Coming. The End-Time worship movement will be led by prophetic music and songs.

10 Sing to the LORD a new song, and His praise
from the ends of the earth, you who go down to the
sea, and all that is in it, you coastlands and you
inhabitants of them! 11 Let the wilderness and its
cities lift up their voice, the villages that Kedar
inhabits. Let the inhabitants of Sela sing, let them
shout from the top of the mountains. 12 Let them
give glory to the LORD, and declare His praise in the
coastlands. 13 The LORD shall go forth like a mighty
man (Jesus' Second Coming); He shall stir up His
zeal like a man of war. He shall cry out, yes, shout
aloud; He shall prevail against His enemies. 14 "I
have held My peace...I have been still and

> *restrained Myself. Now I will cry like a woman in labor, I will pant and gasp at once.15 I will lay waste the mountains and hill (End-Time judgments)..." (Isa. 42:10-15) 16 The Lord will descend from heaven with a shout...and with the trumpet of God...17 We who are alive...shall be caught up together with them in the clouds... (1 Thes. 4:16-17).*

At the end-of-the-age there will be 144,000 prophetic singers from the 5-6 million Jewish intercessors who are described as those who call on God's name in worship and intercession. The 144,000 will stand with Jesus in His government as they sing the new song of the Lord.

> *1 Behold, a Lamb standing on Mount Zion, and with Him 144,000...2 I heard the sound of harpists playing their harps. 3 They sang ...a new song before the Throne...and no one could learn that song except the 144,000 who were redeemed from the earth. (Rev. 14:1-3)*

One of the blessings of going to Israel is the opportunity to see places we read about in the bible and actually put a place with a scripture and see what the scripture is speaking about while you're reading. Such was the case with Mount Zion. It is an actually place right outside of Jerusalem where David built the Tabernacle of David, the first 24/7 place of worship with singing in I Chron. 15-16. So whenever we see Mount Zion in scripture picture the Tabernacle of David. This is what is being referred to here in Rev. 14, the Tabernacle of David on Mount Zion. This is significant for two reasons;

The first significant reason for this is that on Mount Zion in Jerusalem there are actual 24/7 houses of prayer or prayer rooms operating in the city that are Messianic. We were able to pray with them. This was one of the highlights of my trip to Jerusalem; to be able to see this revival. The second significant reason is because in this verse we see that the Lamb stood on Mount Zion, along with the 144,000. It's very possible that I met some of these 144,000. These are Messianic Jews that will worship in the place where David's tabernacle was.

Notice in verse 3, these were redeemed from the earth, meaning they were believers in the Messiah, and were the first fruits for God and the Lamb of those that would come to Yeshua as Messiah. So they are the seed of the Harvest of the salvation of many that are coming to Jesus from the Jews, who will receive Jesus as Messiah.

24/7 Worship with Prayer and evangelism is one of the strategies and expressions of the House of Prayer that will bring this forth, (salvation of all of Israel and the nations, Ro 11:26) and bring Jesus back into the earth. He's going to find a resting place in the city of Jerusalem in the place and presence of 24/7 worship and prayer in earth, as it is in heaven. This is being restored in the earth as we speak in the city of Jerusalem. Furthermore, this is will be final expression of the Gentile Church in the earth as is recorded in the Act 15:14.

14. Simeon has related how God first visited the Gentiles, to take from them a people for his name. 15 And with this the words of the prophets agree, just as it is written, 16"After this I will return, and I will rebuild the tent of David that has fallen; I will rebuild its ruins, and I will restore it, 17that the remnant of mankind may seek the Lord, and all the Gentiles who are called by my name, says the Lord, who makes these things 18 known from of old.'

The Strategy for establishing Cities of Refuge - Worship Prayer and Evangelism

We can see from these verses in Revelation 14 the strategy of God for whole cities that will be turned to Jesus as Messiah at the end of the age. The sixth verse says that an angel flew overhead and delivered unto the 144,000 an eternal gospel to proclaim to those that dwell on the earth. This word *"earth"* is actually speaking of the region in Israel, and specifically the city of Jerusalem. That word "earth" is the word ge – ghay *which means from a primary word; soil; by extension a region, or the solid part or the whole of the terrene globe (including the occupants in each application): - country, earth (-ly), ground, land, world.*

Rev 14:1 Then I looked, and behold, <u>on Mount Zion stood the Lamb</u>, and <u>with him 144,000 who had his name and his Father's name written on their foreheads.</u> 2 And I heard a voice from heaven like the roar of many waters and like the sound of loud thunder. <u>The voice I heard was like the sound of harpists playing on their harps, 3 and they were singing a new song before the throne</u> and before the four living creatures and before the elders. No one could learn that song except the 144,000 who had been redeemed from the earth. 4 <u>It is these who have not defiled themselves with women, for they are virgins. It is these who follow the Lamb wherever he goes.</u> These have been redeemed from mankind as firstfruits for God and the Lamb, 5 and in their mouth no lie was found, for they are blameless.

6 Then I saw another angel flying directly overhead, <u>with an eternal gospel to proclaim to those who dwell on earth, to every nation and tribe and language and people.</u> 7 <u>And he said with a loud voice, "Fear God and give him glory, because the hour of his judgment has come, and worship him who made heaven and earth, the sea and the springs of water."</u> 8 Another angel, a second, followed, saying, "Fallen, fallen is Babylon the great, she

160

who made all nations drink the wine of the passion of her sexual immorality."

The 24/7 Worship, Prayer and Evangelism strategy is not just a good idea or a neat thing to do, it is the strategy of God for the City of Jerusalem and the cities of the earth during times of Judgment in the nations, for Cities of Refuge and cities where whole regions come to Jesus as their Messiah. (***Psalm 122:5-7 during the set times of judgement....Pray for the Peace (reconciliation) of Jerusalem***). There are 6 steps to this strategy of building Cities of Refuge:

1. Eyes to see Jesus in the midst of the Tabernacle David expression of day and night worship and prayer of the Church (called out ones) - *Rev. 14:1*

2. Over 100,000 (OSU Stadium) will come together in a city from the body of Christ, the Lamb, that will be marked and redeemed (set apart) unto the worship of Jesus – *Rev 14:2*

3. A place of worship and prophetic singing that goes up day and night from those who have been marked in the cities of the earth.- *Rev 14:3*

4. The Body of Christ, the Church will come out of Harlot Babylon system and expression of the religious and political system of the earth and they would be pure (virgins) and follow the Lamb (Christ) wherever he leads. *Rev. 14:4*

5. The receiving of the gospel from the messenger Angels to proclaim to those that dwell in the cities of the earth during the times of judgment. – *Rev 14:6*

6. A City-Wide Call to Worship of the God who made heaven and earth. *Rev. 14:7*

The End-Time Church will not be raptured before the Great Tribulation. Rather, the praying Church releases the judgments of the Great Tribulation. God's End-Time judgments will be released by the songs of the redeemed. David prophesied that prophetic worship that will release God's End-Time judgments.

> *6 Let the high praises of God be in their mouth...7 to execute vengeance on the nations, and punishments on the peoples; 8 to bind their kings with chains...9 to execute on them the written judgment-- This honor have all His saints. Praise the LORD! (Ps. 149:6-9)*

The Church at the end of the age will see a great worship movement.

> *14 They shall lift up their voice, they shall sing; for the majesty of the LORD they shall cry aloud from the sea. 15 Therefore glorify the LORD in the dawning light, the name of the LORD God of Israel in the coastlands of the sea. 16 From the ends of the earth we have heard songs: (Isa. 24:14-16)*
> *1 In that day this song will be sung in the land of Judah: "We have a strong city; God will appoint salvation for walls and bulwarks. 2 Open the gates, that the righteous nation which keeps the truth may enter in. (Isa. 26:1-2)*

Step #4: Declare Among the Nations His Doings

The final step in building cities of Refuge from Psalm 9:9-11 are found in declaring among His people His doings, or developing and sharing your prophetic history in God....*declare among the people his doings (v.11).* Scripture exhorts us to remember what God said and did in the past and to teach it to our children. Remembering what God did in our midst helps us to obey and set our hope in Him.

> *² I will open my mouth in a parable; I will utter dark sayings of old, 3 which...our fathers told us...4 telling to the generation to come...His wonderful works. 5 He established a testimony in Jacob...He commanded our fathers, that they should make them known to their children; 6 that the generation to come...may declare them to their children, 7 that they may set their hope in God, and not forget the works of God, but keep His commandments. (Ps. 78:2-7)*

Some of God's ways are given to us as parables that unfold in a way that enables us, as the years go by, to see more and more significance in what He did in the past. Jesus spoke many things in parables to make *truth more clear* to those who were humble and hungry for more and to make *truth more obscure* for those who were proud and spiritually self-satisfied (Mt. 13:3, 13-17).

> *³ He spoke many things to them in parables...13 I speak to them in parables, because seeing they do not see, and hearing they do not hear, nor do they understand. (Mt. 13:3, 13)*

163

Personal prophecy is given to strengthen our resolve to obey God, to be faithful in prayer and to help us keep focused on the specific ministry assignment that God gives us. Prophecy is not a guarantee, but an invitation from God to participate with Him in prayer, faith, and obedience.

> [18] *THIS CHARGE I COMMIT TO YOU, SON TIMOTHY, ACCORDING TO THE PROPHECIES PREVIOUSLY MADE CONCERNING YOU, THAT BY THEM YOU MAY WAGE THE GOOD WARFARE... (1 TIM. 1:18)*

The Father has a vast and glorious storyline for the whole Body of Christ in this generation. He has a specific assignment for each ministry. We all have a small yet significant part to play in His plans. God wants His people to honor and love the whole Church. There is a part of my inheritance in God that I can only receive as I receive from others in the larger Body of Christ. I have been deeply helped through the years by what God has done through other ministries. One such ministry has been IHOP-Kansas City founded by Mike Bickle, where I had the privilege of serving on staff from 2009 to 2012 as an Intercessory Missionary.

IHOP-KC's Prophetic History

IHOP-KC keeps a 24/7 worship sanctuary in obedience to a specific assignment from the Lord. In Cairo, Egypt, September 1982 God spoke these words to Mike Bickle: *I will change the understanding and expression of Christianity in the earth in one generation.*

> *Changing the understanding*: This statement speaks of the way unbelievers will perceive the Church. Today, many see the Church as boring, irrelevant, and non-threatening (Acts 5:11-13).

Changing the expression: This statement speaks of the way the church expresses its life together as a prophetic people of prayer who walk out Sermon on the Mount lifestyles with a forerunner spirit.

God spoke to Mike about *four heart standards* necessary for his future life and ministry. They are not the only values necessary in a New Testament church, but are the *most neglected* ones. In 1996, God corrected his local church, calling them back to these by using the acronym "IHOP."

1. Intercession: night and day prayer and worship affects our *time*

2. Holiness: the Sermon on the Mount lifestyle affects our *thoughts and attitudes*

3. Offerings: extravagant giving by living simply to give more to the harvest affects our *money*

4. Prophetic: confidence in God's intervention (provision, protection, direction) and standing boldly in faith for what the Spirit is saying affects our *security and identity* (most difficult)

The Lord said to Mike, "I am inviting you to be a part of a work that will touch the ends of the earth. You have only said yes, but have not yet done it. Many have said yes, but did not do it (persevere for decades)." The Lord said, "Beware lest your brethren steal these from your heart.

In May 1983, the Lord spoke audibly to Mike, *"I will establish 24-hour prayer in the spirit of the tabernacle of David."* One privilege of keeping a 24/7 worship sanctuary is found in drawing near to God. In engaging in this assignment, we minister to God, release His power, and encounter His heart. In worship and prayer, we contend for a breakthrough of His power on our heart, ministry, and in revelation.

> *[15]But the priests...the sons of Zadok, who kept charge of My sanctuary when the children of Israel went astray from Me, they shall come near Me to minister to Me... (Ezek. 44:15)*

On May 7, 1999, the International House of Prayer of Kansas City (IHOP–KC) began with Mike Bickle and twenty full-time "intercessory missionaries," who cried out to God in prayer with worship for thirteen hours each day. Four months later, on September 19, 1999, prayer and worship extended to the full 24/7 schedule, and has grown from 20 intercessors and singers in a trailer room, to over one thousand full and part-time intercessory missionaries that trust the Lord to provide for their livelihood as missionaries, as they give themselves, like Anna (Luke 2:38-40) continually, to day and night to prayer, fasting, worship and works of Justice in their community.

IHOP–KC is an evangelical missions organization that is committed to praying for the release of the fullness of God's power and purpose, while actively winning the lost, healing the sick, feeding the poor, making disciples, and impacting every sphere of society—family, education, government, economy, arts, media, religion, etc. The vision of IHOP-KC is to work in relationship with the Body of Christ to serve the Great Commission, while seeking to walk out the two great commandments to love God and people. The Lord has called IHOP-KC to be a community of believers committed to God, each other, and to establishing a 24/7 house of prayer in Kansas City—a perpetual solemn assembly gathering corporately to fast and pray, in the spirit of the tabernacle of David. The Holy Spirit is orchestrating *one great move of God* in this generation. It is comprised of *many smaller ministry movements* that each has a specific ministry assignment. In other words, the end-time prayer movement is made up of many smaller prayer movements. IHOP–KC is one small movement in the midst of the global end-time move of God.

In Declaring Among the Nations what God did in IHOP–KC's "prophetic history," this represents a very small part of God's story in this generation. In telling the prophetic history of IHOP-KC, my prayer is that part of IHOP-KC's story will encourage you to believe God for His fullness in your ministry assignment, and position you to declare among the nations all that God does as you follow God's specific assignment for your life. As each ministry does their small part, others see the big picture of God's puzzle a little more clearly. In chapter 2 I shared some of my own personal testimony and prophetic history in declaring what God did in my own life and ministry, of how God brought me into this movement of 24/7 worship with prayer in the earth, for the building of a City of Refuge in my own City of Columbus Ohio.

CHAPTER 10

THE VISION OF FEED MY SHEEP FOOD & CLOTHING STORE AND THE END OF THE AGE DYNAMICS

As I shared in the Introduction, I believe our society and economic system (a debtor society) is headed within the next few years in our nation to a complete economic and financial collapse. We will not get out of the mess that this system of debt in our country has gotten us in without a complete collapse of the system. We must wake up fast and stop following the lead of this debtor system, as well as our political leaders and their bankrupt solutions. In the Body of Christ we must take our cue from the ants of Proverbs 6:7, which have no leaders but they store up food during harvest. Proverbs 6:1-7 says;

> *My son, if you have put up security for your neighbor, if you have shaken hands in pledge for a stranger, you have been trapped by what you said, ensnared by the words of your mouth. So do this, my son, to free yourself, since you have fallen into your neighbor's hands: Go—to the point of exhaustion—and give your neighbor no rest! Allow no sleep to your eyes, no slumber to your eyelids. Free yourself, like a gazelle from the hand of the hunter, like a bird from the snare of the fowler. Go to the ant, you sluggard; consider its ways and be wise! It has no commander, no overseer or ruler, yet it stores its provisions in summer and gathers its food at harvest. How long will you lie there, you sluggard? When will you get up from your sleep? A little sleep, a little slumber, a little folding of the*

> *hands to rest— and poverty will come on you like a*
> *thief and scarcity like an armed man*

Verse 4 says, allow no sleep to your eyes, no slumber to your eyelids, free yourself like a gazelle from the hand of the hunter, like a bird from the snare of the fowler. Then verse 5 says, go to the ant, you sluggard: consider its way and be wise. It has no commander, no overseer or ruler, yet it stores its provisions in the summer and gathers its food at harvest.

My Pre-Tribulation Rapture Quandry

God is positioning Intercessors, watchmen, and forerunner messengers in His house of prayer to transition His church for this coming day of Judgment and revival in our nation and world. He's going to cause His church to be covered, protected and provided for supernaturally during this time. And not only that but God is going to raise up His church to possess the wealth of the nations for the preservation of His chosen people Israel, during this coming shaking in the earth. For years I had grappled within my soul with the feeling that God wanted to use the Church to assist and minister to His chosen people, the Jews, during the time of their greatest shaking and Judgment, called "Jacob's trouble" (Jeremiah 30:5, 6). One night I had a dream that I was in the midst of what looked like what I had heard taught in my Church growing up as, *"The Great Tribulation."* And I was given a mandate to start a grocery store to feed Christians and Jews food during a great drought, food shortage and economic collapse. When I awoke I was terrified because I thought, "Oh no, It must be that I'm going to fall away from the Lord in the future and be *Left Behind.* The book series by Tim Lahaye, by that title *"Left Behind"* had recently been released. I could never reconcile that dream with the teachings I had learned of the pre-tribulation rapture, where it was taught that we would be caught away to miss this mess coming in the earth, at a time when Israel was going through the time of Jacob's trouble, and when they would need us the most. I grew up in a traditional Pentecostal church, so my view was shaped by this pre-tribulation rapture perspective. In fact, so much so, that it even affected the way I interpreted this dream from God. But God began showing me another theological viewpoint concerning the rapture, called Historic Pre-millennialism with a victorious church going through the Great Tribulation with great power, provision and victory.

Historic Pre-millennialism with a Victorious Church

This theological view combines the biblical strengths of postmillennialism and amillennialism with historic pre-millennialism, and the call to victory and wholeheartedness.

In this view a victorious Church attains to reconciliation, unity, intimacy, and maturity, resulting in the greatest revival in history (Eph. 4:13). This prophetic praying Church will walk in great power and supernatural provision, as it is used to bring in the end-time harvest and to transform society in various places.

In this view a wholehearted Church walks in "Sermon on the Mount lifestyles" of self-denial and serving, giving, blessing, praying, and fasting as seen in the New Testament Church (Mt. 5-7). This lifestyle will be energized by encountering Jesus as the Bridegroom God (Rev. 22:17).

In this view a relevant Church sees the continuity of some of our labors in impacting society now (righteous legislation, education, etc.) with the work of Jesus in the Millennium. All that is unrighteous will be dismantled and then re-established in righteousness in the Millennium. However, righteous legislation in society in this age will not need to be replaced. Works in society built on godliness and justice will last beyond the shaking of the tribulation judgments.

Being a part of a ministry for years that taught a pre-trib rapture I felt I could not be truthful on what I believed concerning the end-times because I didn't want to bring division in the church between the Pastor's view and the view God was revealing to me. After God led me to connect with IHOP-KC, I was in a service where the speaker, a young man by the name of Benji Nolot, was speaking on the subject of the *"Timing of the Rapture."* It felt like I was being allowed to breathe freely for the first time in over 10 years, as the speaker begin to articulate the mysteries that God had been revealing to my heart, that I had held in for so many years.

When the Rapture will Occur

The big question that has been debated for the better part of the last 100 years is: when will the rapture take place? This is the question I had to have answered for myself to be able to understand what God was showing me in preparing for this *Day of the Lord.* For many, the answer to this question is a foregone conclusion. Typically people's view differs based on what stream of the Body of Christ in which they were raised. There is almost a universal conviction among pre-millennial scholars that the final week of Daniel is the time frame that concludes this age. In other words, human history in this age will end with a unique seven-year period of time. The discussion concerning the rapture involves discerning at what point before, during, or after this seven years the rapture occurs.

Views on the rapture

There are four different views on the timing of the rapture according to those who subscribe to pre-millennial eschatology.

Pre-tribulation – Views the rapture as occurring seven years before Jesus' Second Coming.

Mid-tribulation – Views the rapture as occurring 3 ½ years before Jesus' Second Coming. **Pre-wrath** – Views the rapture as occurring at an undefined period of time after the 3½-year mark of the Tribulation and before the end of the Tribulation. This view sees the rapture as occurring at the sixth seal in the book of Revelation (Rev. 6:12-17).

Post-tribulation – Views the rapture as occurring after the Tribulation at the Second Coming of Jesus.

How many "comings" of Jesus and "resurrections" of the saints are there? – Three of these views (pre-trib, mid-trib, and pre-wrath) stand or fall on the basis of two basic premises: 1) Are there two Second Comings of Christ? 2) Are there two resurrections of the saints? If it can be accurately shown that there are, then distinguishing when the rapture occurs would be extremely difficult, and basically be an arbitrary judgment. If there is not, then these views are inconclusive and ultimately the product of mere speculation. In my observation and understanding of Scripture there is no explicit evidence to support the conclusion that there are two, separate Second Coming events, nor two resurrections of the saints. The best place for us to begin to answer the question "when does the rapture occur?" is by identifying what we know to be true about the Second Coming and the rapture. The five truths I am going to present directly contrast three of the four rapture views.

The Second Coming is a Singular Event Occurring After the Tribulation

"Immediately after the tribulation of those days the sun will be darkened, and the moon will not give its light; the stars will fall from heaven, and the powers of the heavens will be shaken. Then the sign of the Son of Man will appear in heaven, and then all the tribes of the earth will mourn, and they will see the Son of Man coming on the clouds of heaven with power and great glory. And He will send His angels with a great sound of a trumpet, and they will gather together His elect from the four winds, from one end of heaven to the other." – Mt. 24:29-31

Jesus describes His Second Coming as a singular event occurring after the tribulation. At no point in His teaching ministry does he ever reference another time frame for His return. After His resurrection Jesus spent forty days with His disciples. When He finally ascended into heaven two angels appeared to the disciples and informed them: "This same Jesus, who was taken up from you into heaven, will so come in like manner as you saw Him go into heaven." (Acts 1:11) The angels described a singular event in which Jesus would come back from heaven to the earth. Some point to 1 Thes. 4:15-18 to validate a view that Jesus Christ returns momentarily in the sky to rapture the church seven years before His Second Coming. However, there is no doubt that Paul's views were formed by Christ's teachings. If he was introducing a new view concerning a subject as important as an entirely separate Second Coming event, I imagine he would have said so. Paul's teaching harmonizes perfectly with what Jesus taught in the Olivet Discourse.

> *For this we say to you by the word of the Lord, that we who are alive, and remain [perileipomenoi] until the coming of the Lord will by no means precede those who are asleep. For the Lord Himself will descend from heaven with a shout, with the voice of an archangel, and with the trumpet of God. And the dead in Christ will rise first. Then we who are alive and remain [perileipomenoi] shall be caught up together with them in the clouds to meet the Lord in the air. And thus we shall always be with the Lord. Therefore comfort one another with these words.* – 1 Thes. 4:15-18.

Nowhere in the text is precedence given for a time frame other than the one already established by Jesus. Consider the parallels in the two passages: In Matthew 24 we see that Christ is descending from heaven with angels and a trumpet gathering together His followers. In 1Thess 4 we see that Christ is descending from heaven with angels and a trumpet, gathering together His followers. The noun used for the word "come" (parousia) in the NT means arrival or presence. The verb tense of this word implies continuous and progressive action. When Jesus returns, He is coming to establish His manifest presence and initiate an indefinite mission upon the earth.

Any position subscribing to a view that necessitates two Second Coming events is rooted in theory not Scripture. This is an important distinction to make. Nowhere does the Bible delineate between two separate Second Coming events. However the Bible does emphatically describe one event, which occurs after the Tribulation, not at any point before it.

The Rapture Occurs After the Tribulation

"Immediately after the tribulation of those days the sun will be darkened, and the moon will not give its light; the stars will fall from heaven, and the powers of the heavens will be shaken. Then the sign of the Son of Man will appear in heaven, and then all the tribes of the earth will mourn, and they will see the Son of Man coming on the clouds of heaven with power and great glory. And He will send His angels with a great sound of a trumpet, and they will gather (episynago) together His elect from the four winds, from one end of heaven to the other." – Mt. 24:29-31

Jesus describes the rapture as an event that is synonymous with His Second Coming. The apostle Paul also describes the Second Coming and the rapture as one synonymous event.

"Now, brethren, concerning the coming of our Lord Jesus Christ and our gathering (episynago) together to Him..." – 2 Thess. 2:1

Both Jesus and Paul use the same word for "gather," episynago. The only explicit time frame given to understand the return of Christ and the rapture of the saints is "after the tribulation." If the rapture occurs after the tribulation what does that mean? It means the Church is here during the tribulation. Jesus, in fact, prefigures the presence of believers during the tribulation.

"Therefore when you see the 'abomination of desolation'... And pray that your flight may not be in the winter or on the Sabbath. For then there will be great tribulation, since has not been since the beginning of the world until this time, no, nor ever

> *shall be... Then if anyone says to you, 'Look, here is the Christ!' or 'There!' do not believe it... Therefore if they say to you, 'Look, He is in the desert!' do not go out... For as the lightning comes from the east and flashes to the west, so also will the coming of the Son of Man be." (Mt. 24:15,20-21, 23, 26-27)*

The clear emphasis of Jesus' teaching prefigured the presence of believers on earth during the Great Tribulation. Dispensationalists would speculate that Jesus was speaking to Jews here, and so it is the Jews who will be present during the tribulation, while the Church has been raptured. If one consistent with their logic then they must at least acknowledge it is "believing" Jews who Jesus is speaking to. So are we now meant to understand that though the church has been raptured, Jewish believers are left behind because of their ethnicity? Are they then not members of the Church? This train of logic is a theological train wreck. I do not have time in this chapter to develop how preposterous this scenario is. The fact is that Jesus is preparing the leaders of His Church with important information pertaining to their survival during the great tribulation.

Believers are also pictured as present during the Great Tribulation throughout the book of Revelation. Once again dispensationalists would redefine this truth by pointing out that though the term "saints" is used, the word "ecclesia" or Church is not used in Rev. 4-19. Their conclusion then is that the Church must not be here and that the saints that are written about are a new group of believers who were saved during the Tribulation but are not members of the Church.

Once again the logic employed here is not consistent. Revelation 4-19 illustrates what is occurring on earth AND in heaven. If the term ecclesia is the technical word that we use to decipher the presence or lack thereof of the church, and the conclusion is that

177

since ecclesia isn't used in Rev. 4-19 the Church cannot be on the earth, then doesn't it stand to reason that the Church cannot be in heaven either? This presents an irreconcilable quandary, and therefore cannot be considered tenable.

Indeed the term ecclesia is not the technical word by which we decipher the presence of the Church. In fact six New Testament epistles do not use the term ecclesia (2 Tim., Titus, 1 & 2 Peter, 2 John, and Jude) but do use the term saints, a term used throughout the book of Revelation. Even more striking, the word Church is also missing from those passages directly dealing with the rapture when Christians see Jesus again (Jn. 14:1; 1 Cor. 15; 1 Thes. 4-5). It is not even in the description of the new heaven and new earth or the New Jerusalem (Rev. 21-22). You can read more concerning the rapture of the church in my book, "Upon this Rock, I will Build My Church," in the chapter, *"The Timing of the Rapture"*

The Vision of Feed My Sheep Food & Clothing Store & Cities of Refuge

Concerning this dream that I had, I was in the midst of the Great Tribulation and I was given a mandate to start a grocery store to feed Christians food during the shaking of the nations of the earth's financial and economic systems. In the dream the vision of this store was to be a Christian grocery store that doesn't operate on the monetary system of the world, but operates as a grocery store just the same.

Though the store would be set up just like a grocery store with quality food and clothes, with tags and prices on all items, the only prerequisite for Christian shoppers would be a weekly voucher received as a result of church attendance/membership with a church affiliated with Feed My Sheep Food and Clothing Store. Unbelievers that would seek to shop at Feed My Sheep would notice heavily discounted prices in comparison to the worlds markets without compromising quality. Christian shoppers that would shop at FMS would be asked to simply give a donation. Our aim would be to provide for the needs of the body of Christ and the needy of the world by obeying Jesus' command to "FEED MY SHEEP" and to present the gospel of Jesus Christ to the world through the message and method of Love in action. This will be accomplished by manifesting the compassion that Christ did when he fed the 5000 with the two fish and five loaves. It was this compassion that was instrumental in producing the miracle of the multiplication of the loaves and the fish. And it is this compassion that will be instrumental in providing miraculously for the needs, supplies and operational expenses of the body of Christ during this time of the shortage of food through Feed My Sheep. (FMS)

Not a Food Pantry

It is the aim of FMS to be a grocery /clothing store exclusively for those who are seeking to be set apart unto the kingdom of God, not just a food pantry or thrift store for the needy. The only prerequisite for shopping at FMS however will be Church attendance where the gospel of the kingdom is being preached. Shoppers will be able to receive vouchers from one of the daily/weekly services at the House of Prayer missions' bases in that city, or the other churches affiliated with the store throughout the city. Those that do not attend a participating church will receive a voucher upon their initial visit to the store and a brochure and an invitation to the church nearest them. After that initial visit to FMS they will be required to attend a prayer/worship service to receive their next voucher to be able to shop at the store. If they haven't attended a service after their initial voucher visit they will be required to pay the prices that are listed on the items desired. Because our aim will be to have quality items, not just second hand stuff, we will be looking to draw the world to the store and to the gospel of the Kingdom of

179

God. All ministries or social agencies that utilize the food and clothing store as a referral for their members will be required to pay a membership fee and become a monthly partner, donating monthly to the upkeep and operational expenses of the store. With this vision we will be positioned within the church, in neighborhoods and cities to establish CITIES OF REFUGE, and POCKETS OF MERCY, during hard economic times coming to our nation and world at the end of the age.

CHAPTER 11

BUILDING "ACTS 4 COMMUNITIES" FOR ECONOMIC AND FINANCIAL PROVISION & WEALTH TRANSFER

"And all that believed were together, and had all things common; and they sold their possessions and goods, and parted them to all men, as every man had need.....Neither was there any among them that lacked. (Acts 2:44-46; Acts 4:31-35)

I believe God wants to return the body of Christ to *First Century* agricultural and financial models of provision, supply and wealth-building seen in the early Church, when they lived with all things in common, from within *"Acts 4 Communities,"* seen and recorded in the book of Acts, chapters 2 through 4 in scripture. It was seen in these communities in scripture, after the day of Pentecost, a whole network of believers who came together through daily times of prayer, fellowship and breaking of bread, to network, sell and share their goods with one another.

The Spirit of Wisdom for Our Times

I believe God wants to release Acts 4-type wisdom to the body of Christ over the next few years to prepare His church for a First Century Church type famine in the earth, as was seen Acts 11:27-30. As Joseph, the body of Christ has been enslaved in this world's debtor system, but God wants to raise His people up to become the head and not the tail. He wants to take us from the pit to the palace. I believe this will be one of the things that will come out of this coming economic and financial fall-out. Through prophetic messages, encouraging the Church to begin storing up food outside of the world markets, I believe the Church is being positioned to survive, as well as thrive during these times, just as Joseph in Genesis 42, and just as the first century Church in Acts 11:27-30;

> *And in these days came prophets from Jerusalem unto Antioch. 28 And there stood up one of them named Agabus, and signified by the Spirit that there should be great dearth throughout all the world: which came to pass in the days of Claudius Caesar. 29 Then the disciples, every man according to his ability, determined to send relief unto the brethren which dwelt in Judaea: 30 Which also they did, and sent it to the elders by the hands of Barnabas and Saul.*

These days of great dearth from the *First Century Church* are coming upon us again in the *Last Century Church*. I believe the wisdom of God being released into the earth, ahead of these times to come, will not be conventional wisdom. It won't make sense to the carnal, natural mind. It might not seem like the thing to do. But it will be the key that unlocks financial increase and wealth transfer for the body of Christ. This wisdom will be outside of the traditional, conventional systems from the present corporate way of operating and hiring employees that is presently the predominant economic systems of operation in the earth. This wisdom will produce unconventional means of provision, livelihood, and wealth-building during a time when resources and jobs are scarce.

God is about to return the body of Christ to *First Century* agricultural and financial models of provision, supply and wealth-building seen in the early Church, when they lived with all things in common, from within *"Acts 4 Communities,"* seen and recorded in the book of Acts, chapters 2 through 4 in scripture. It was seen in these communities in scripture, after the day of Pentecost, a whole network of believers who came together through daily times of prayer, fellowship and breaking of bread, to network, sell and share their goods with one another. *"And all that believed were together, and had all things common;* **and they sold their possessions and goods, and parted them to all men, as every man had need.....**<u>**Neither was there any among them that lacked.**</u> (Acts 2:44-46; Acts 4:31-35)

Sold and Parted their Possessions and Goods

Acts 4 says they *"sold"* their possessions and goods and *"parted"* them to all men, as every man had need. I believe that these verses, recorded in Acts 2 and 4, sets forth more than a communal system of socialist's theology to put everybody on the same economic plain. There is wisdom in these verses that will give the body of Christ keys to *Arise during the Coming Financial Fall.* Firstly, these verses are not just speaking of selling any goods and possessions. The word "goods" and "possessions" in this passage comes from a Greek word that means natural resources or natural wealth, like gold, silver, cattle, coffee, or natural energy like coal, etc, that come from the earth. These are the types of resources that are naturally valuable, wealth generators. These are the types of resources the first century church sold and parted. Most people know what it means to sell their goods, but few know it means to part your goods. The scripture says they *"parted"* their goods to all men.

That word *"Parted"* is not just referring to sharing their goods, it's actually more closely related to what we know today as networking. When you put "selling" their goods together with "parting" their goods to all men," you have a first century picture of the current direct sells, network marketing industry that has become increasing popular over the last decade with the rise of the internet and social networking. They sold their goods

183

amongst themselves and promoted each other's resource of choice, multiplying their efforts through discipleship marketing. This is marketing through relationship-building, through word of mouth selling of goods amongst themselves, so that none lacked among them. For example, they didn't just fish and sell their fish, but they *"Parted"* them, which means, in addition to selling their fish, they taught those interested in making a living fishing, to fish and sell the fish they caught, and the teacher received a portion back – like a tithe or less - from what they sold, to multiply their efforts, increasing the quality of life for all, not just themselves.

The Networking System of the Kingdom of God

I believe these verses are referring to what we see the last generation returning to, with the rise of the internet and social networking craze. With the present rise of the (MLM) Network Marketing/Direct sales industry steadily increasing, becoming more prevalent over the last decades in the earth, I believe God is setting before the body of Christ a *First century* system of operation in this generation for us to consider and live by at the end of age as the world's economic systems began to fail and collapse. Could this be the system being placed before us as the mechanism for divine provision and supply for His church, along with the redistribution of wealth for kingdom advancement? Is it possible that God could be setting in place for His Church the networking systems for implementation, so that we not only survive when the world's economies fail, but that we thrive during these times?

The MLM System of Wealth-Building

Many within the body of Christ have overlooked this Multi-Level Marketing (*MLM*) industry, or allowed the secular media and entertainment to capitalize on the social networking craze, and have not considered that this could be God's wisdom and mechanism for the release of unity and the commanded blessing on the Church at the end of the age. Many have dismissed this MLM industry as a get rich quick pyramid scheme. But as the noted author of *Rich Dad, Poor Dad*, Robert Kiyosaki states, *"The network marketing and direct sales industry is recognized by many to be the fastest-growing business model in the world today. Many people still have a negative reaction, claiming that many network marketing organizations are pyramid schemes. Yet in reality, the biggest pyramid scheme in the world is the traditional business corporation, with one person at the top and all the workers below. I speak favorably of the Network Marketing/Direct Sales industry, because this model provides essential sales, business-building and leadership skills not found anywhere else.*

Even though Robert Kiyosaki is the foremost financial author in the world for generating unconventional wealth in changing financial times, I'm not just taking his word for it. My investigation, study and paradigm shift to this model as a strategy for the body of Christ for wealth building and wealth transfer is not just because of what Robert Kiyosaki has to say about it, I believe this model could be a strategy for the body of Christ at the end of the age because of what Jesus had to say about it. Network, Multi-Level Marketing/Direct Sales is the model Jesus implemented in building His church long before there were printed adds, hand-bills, flyers, bill-boards, radios, televisions, or internet to market and sale product. Jesus took twelve men and mentored them in the techniques of sharing one on one, face to face (*direct-selling*) the product of the good news of the Kingdom of God. Then He sent them out two by two and told them to be fruitful and *exponentially* multiply what He put in them; *Go ye into the all the world and make disciples of all nations. (Matt 28:19)* From those initial twelve disciples there has been a compounding residual return on His initial 3 and 1 half years of investing into these men that has birthed a world-wide movement called the

Church, which has grown exponentially and generationally for the past 2000 years.

Generational Exponential Wealth

This model and system of network marketing or relational, word-of-mouth marketing is alive and well in this social networking generation. It's not only alive and well, but this relational, networking system that produces compounding, residual income is the wealth generating system that releases the product and proceeds to succeeding generations. This is how Jesus' Church and work has been growing and compounding exponentially for over 2000 years, while he only worked it for 3 and 1 half years. In addition to that, I believe it could very well be how wealth will be extracted from an old, dying economic system which has continually grown corrupt and has ultimately been a vehicle to oppress the masses, producing a ruling class and an under-class – *A Pyramid.*

As we see the kingdom of God coming, we can see this present corporate, non-relational economic system operating in the earth passing away as we steadily approach the end of the age. And it is my belief that it will have its final death and funeral after the coming forth and overthrowing of the One-World Babylonian, Anti-Christ system. This coming One-World financial order is the system I believe will arise out of the coming collapse of the present economic systems and models existing and operating today.

This present economic system is a system of debt meant to trap the body of Christ and the whole world in an inescapable web of deceitfulness of riches. This system is in the process of drawing in as many people, nations and systems as can be drawn in, to close and clamp down on its subjects to make slaves of the whole human race. As we seek God's wisdom and divine strategies for

186

our deliverance from this system God is going to begin to raise up many that will operate as end-time Josephs in the earth to preserve and prosper the body of Christ at the end of the age, at a time when the whole world and its economic systems are rocking and reeling. If we act now to free ourselves from this system of debt and begin preparing for the collapse of this system, by operating by another standard and system, and by learning to handle our money by the principles of the word of God, as well as by storing up food and living essentials, we will not only avoid this great disaster coming from this fallout, but we will arise to see a great harvest of souls and transfer of wealth come into our hands. Proverbs says how long we will lie here doing nothing? Sleep a little, doze a little, fold our hands a little and twiddle your thumbs. Suddenly, everything is gone, as though it had been taken by an armed robber (Proverbs 6:11).

CHAPTER 12

THE TWELVE CITY PROPHECIES

The Coming Forth of Transformational Communities in our Nation

Intercessory prayer will be instrumental in releasing divine provision and supernatural crops, food and rain during the time of drought all around us. In my book, The Melchizedek Priesthood of Jesus Christ, I share how Abraham's encounter with the priest of the Most High God, Melchizedek, in the land of Canaan in Genesis 14, undoubtedly left a major impartation in that geographical region of the earth. The fruit of Canaan was many times the regular size of crops in other regions. I shared how the release of the revelation and impartation of the Melchizedek Priesthood of intercessory prayer in the last days to reconcile heaven and earth will leave a major impartation in the key regions of the earth that God will raise up as cities of refuge during the coming times of shaking in the earth. During this time supernatural crops will grow during times of drought. Fruit and vegetables three and four times the size of the average will grow during times of famine. Rain will be released in these regions in the middle of drought all around us. These cities will be characterized by revival centers of prayer, worship and fasting, seeking God day and night, where God's power will be released transcending the church buildings and church services, pouring out into the society and the earth in those regions which will be known as *"Pockets of Mercy."*

George Otis and the Transformational Communities Documentaries

Some regions around the world are already experiencing these unique and unusual out-pours that affect the earth and crops in those regions. Film maker George Otis has captured many of these instances in other regions of the world, in documentaries called; *TRANSFORMATIONAL COMMUNITIES.*

Imagine a community where 92 percent of the population is born-again; where city jails have been closed for lack of crime; where agricultural productivity has reached biblical proportions. Imagine a city where 60,000 Christians jam the municipal soccer stadium for all-night prayer vigils every 90 days; where a multi-billion dollar drug cartel has been brought to its knees. Don't imagine... believe! George Otis, Jr. has documented these transformed communities on three continents. These documentaries are just snapshots of what God wants to do in the in key cities throughout the earth, and how the power of prayer can deliver similar results in your own neighborhood.

Prophecy Concerning Regions of Revival and Pockets of Mercy

Many Prophets within the body of Christ have already been dealt with about cities where God's spirit will be poured out in unique and unusual ways that could very well be these Cities of Refuge during this coming day of the Lord. A prophet by the name of Bob Jones, along with several other noted prophets in the body of Christ were shown 12 cities where these and similar outpourings would begin breaking out, igniting the fires of Revival. Bob said, *"An angel showed me that it would begin in Kansas City, and that God will send great finances to Kansas City and that it will be a city where people will form a partnership with God, and let Him do*

190

with His money as He chooses. Great famines will be seen around the world. Kansas City will be a world shipping center for grain. It will export both natural and spiritual bread. I asked the Lord how this could be and He said over and over, "It will be because those that pray will receive from My hand. Intercession will release natural rain and great mercy. God is raising up a people in Kansas City who will pray so that the rains will come." The angel showed me other cities in the US that will have an unusual measure of protection and blessing. (We refer to areas like this as "pockets of mercy.")

The other prophet that was given a prophecy about 12 cities in America that would be revival hubs was Rick Joyner. Both Rick Joyner and Bob Jones have been shown separate visions about not one city, but 12 cities in America that would become Revival Hubs. Rick actually published an article in 1992, titled; "The Twelve City Prophecy" based on an encounter that he had on February 6, 1989. This article was published in the MorningStar Journal Vol. 2, No. 3 and again in Vol. 11, No. 1.

The 12 Cities of the 12 City Prophecies

The other prophet that had the same 12 city vision was Todd Bentley. In Lakeland he was given a promise of how the ark of God and Revival would be carried from city to city. This fire would be transferrable. It would be a tangible fire. People could take it back to their nation and their city. In praying for this, the Lord began to have Todd revisit the original prophetic promise of the 12 cities that he was given to Bob in April of 2008. The Lord asked him, *"Do you remember that word?"* He said, *"Yes Lord."* He then said, **"That word is for now. This 12-city promise is for now. You need to fire it up again, and you need to focus specifically on praying for people from Ohio and keep prophesying Ohio. He said watch Ohio, because as it breaks there, it is going to begin to break in many other cities."**

Here are the 12 cities that Todd Bentley was given in April 2008:

1. Lakeland/Orlando, Florida (Lakeland Outpouring)
2. Charlotte, NC ("Breakout" happened at Morning-Star)
3. Kansas City, MO (Student Awakening)
4. Ohio
5. Atlanta, GA
6. Des Moines, Iowa
7. Omaha and Lincoln, Nebraska
8. Dallas/Ft. Worth, TX
9. Denver, CO
10. Nashville, TN
11. Portland/Albany, OR
12. Seattle, WA

Todd then said he thought, God why did you name all of these specific cities, but when it came to Ohio the promise was "Ohio" After this, He was speaking with Bob Jones and Todd said, *"Bob I think we need to release this."* And Bob said, *"Did you know a friend of mine, Bonnie, had an angelic encounter March 1 and the Lord came to her and spoke to her about Ohio?"* And He said, *"Really?" "In fact Todd, you didn't know this, but just today Bonnie came to me and asked me if Ohio was one of the 12 cities. And now you are coming to me with Ohio."* About this time, Rick joined the conversation, and shared how he had published a similar encounter called the 12-city prophecy. Now, up to that time Todd had never read or heard of this prophecy prior to this conversation. Rick shared how in regards to Ohio, *"in the vision I saw an actual map of the U.S. with these cities marked as points. I did not know all of the cities and had to look them up on an Atlas." I have a question mark by Columbus, Ohio which I do in this article because I actually saw the entire state of Ohio being highlighted, and I put down Columbus with a question mark because it is kind of in the center and I thought maybe it would be centered there.* **But I got the same thing, the entire state of Ohio.** *There is something about that.* **You are going to see something remarkable happen in Ohio. God told Bob in 2008, this word is for now. This 12-city promise is for now.**

Columbus Ohio - A City Of Refuge

Rev 21:2 And I John saw the holy city, new Jerusalem, coming down from God out of heaven, prepared as a bride adorned for her husband.

It was 1992 after a Holy Land tour to Jerusalem that God first placed in my heart a burden for my city Columbus Ohio and the people of my city. He had shown me His burden for Jerusalem and the strife and struggle between the two brothers from Abraham – *Isaac and Ishmael* – and He told me when I returned home that the answer to the burden of His heart for Jerusalem and the people of the City of God was to go home and learn to live together as opposites in my own city – *Husband with Wife, Black with White, Rich with Poor, Baptist with Apostolic, etc, in the nations of the earth.*

God save our City Nation and World

That's when God began to give me a love and a vision for Columbus Ohio, to see my city saved. That's when God supernaturally took out of my heart any hint of bitterness, or strife, anger against another race of people, that's when God gave me a compassion for the poor and discarded in life, and that's when God began to send me out saying, *"Feed My Sheep."* It was at that time in 1993, from a store front church in the ghetto of Columbus Ohio, with no money and very few people, that I began reaching out to my City doing tent Crusades, called *"God Save our City, Nation and World Crusades."* I felt God saying, that by reaching out to one neighborhood at a time with My love and

193

compassion in this city, you'll see revival hit Columbus Ohio, and City by City you'll see and bring peace and prosperity to the Nation, and Nation by Nation, you'll bring peace and prosperity to the World – Culminating in a Worldwide crusade in Jerusalem that will consummate in the coming of the Lord.

With this burden and vision in hand I began to reach out to the City of Columbus Ohio seeking to know the purpose and calling of my City. In prayer God gave me this vision, mission and goal statement for God Save Our City Crusades, along with the following method of restoring the Love for God and our neighbor in our inner city neighborhoods, *PUTTING THE NEIGHBOR BACK IN THE HOOD.*

This was the original vision, mission, purpose and goal statement given 15 years ago when I returned from Israel, with a few alterations added since that time. As I submitted my life and vision to this vision God gave me the mantle of the City, and the vision of replacing the crown of pride over our City with the crown of Glory (Isaiah 28) over our City of Columbus Ohio, taking authority back from the spirits of Leviathan operating in the City, and establishing the Lordship of Jesus Christ.

In 2008 God moved me, and brought me into relationship with Lou Engel, Mike Bickle and the International House of Prayer in Kansas City Missouri, showing me the pattern and blueprint for bringing the prayer movement and the end-time evangelism movement together to release a world-wide revival of the pouring out of God's spirit once again upon all flesh.

The Calling and Purpose of Our Cities
The New Columbus

Once I begin reaching out in my city of Columbus Ohio in 2003, God allowed me to gain access to the City of Columbus Ohio's official vision, mission, goal statement that is disseminated to governmental city officials. And much to my surprise it coincided with what God had spoken to me was His heart and vision for this City. Remember, every city has a purpose and a calling, and it is in the fulfillment of this purpose and calling that a city becomes a Holy City. Once we received this vision, mission and goal statement of Columbus Ohio and realized that it was the mind of God for this city, we began to declare it, decree it and pray it into the heavens over the city, to lay the foundations of the earth, that He might say unto Columbus, *"You are my people."* (Isaiah 51:16,17). Below, in italicized capital lettering are the vision, mission and goal statements, along with the principles of progress for Columbus Ohio, which I received from the Mayor's office, with a few points that we added to focus in on this City becoming a City of Refuge, a Holy City, and a New Columbus.

Vision of Columbus Ohio

Father we declare Columbus will be saved *and it will be the best city in the nation in which to live, work, and raise a family.*

Mission of Columbus Ohio

Columbus will provide leadership that will inspire: high standards of excellence in the delivery of city services; Columbus will have a spirit of cooperation, pride and responsibility to achieve strong, safe and healthy neighborhoods; and, a shared economic prosperity and enhanced quality of life. We undertake this mission

195

believing and knowing that we can make a difference for future generations.

Principles of progress for Columbus Ohio

Our city will be prepared for the next generation.

Our city will promote a diverse and vibrant economy that offers everyone an opportunity to share in our prosperity.

Our city will deliver measurable, quality public services and results to our residents.

Our city will advance our neighborhoods in all ethnicities, races and cultures in this city.

The races of our city will be united and work in unity and harmony.

Our city will be challenged to realize its promise and potential.

Goals of Columbus Ohio

Our city will provide quality and efficient service delivery to customers using "best practices".

Our city will engage and promote strong, distinct, and vibrant neighborhoods.

Our city will enhance the delivery of safety services.
Our city will provide an atmosphere that promotes job creation and economic growth in existing and emerging industries.

Our city will encourage and promote participation in learning opportunities.

Our city will develop a vibrant and thriving downtown that is recognized as an asset for the region.

Our city will invest in all city employees and develop systems that support a high-performing city government.

Love the Lord thy God...And thy Neighbor as Thyself

After the launching of God Save Our City Crusades In September 2003 I've received the answer to my question that I asked God on the balcony of the Jerusalem Hilton. Remember he spoke to me saying, if you want to know the answer to the middle east dilemma concerning the key to living in peace and harmony, he said, *"you go home and learn how to live together man and wife, black and white, rich and poor in your family and community, learn how to live together, the head of the body, and the members of the body in the church, and you'll receive the answer and solution to the Jewish, Arab dilemma."*

Well, since 2003 I have come to the understanding and received a revelation from his word that, *"the key to living in peace and harmony in the earth with husband, and wife, black and white, rich and poor, in community as well as in the church is, learning how to live out of the fruit of the spirit of love, with your flesh subject to the spirit of God.* This is what has been revealed to me the key to transforming a church, transforming a neighborhood and community, transforming a city and a nation. The fruit of the spirit of love!

> *Luke 10:27 love the lord thy god with all they heart, mind and strength and love thy neighbor as thy self.*

197

Having the Glory of God in Our Cities

Rev 21:11 having the glory of god: and her light was like unto a stone most precious, even like a jasper stone, clear as crystal;

Rev 21:12 and had a wall great and high, and had twelve gates, and at the gates twelve angels, and names written thereon, which are the names of the twelve tribes of the children of Israel:

1. The Glory Of God, which in revelation 21:11 is likened unto a stone most precious, even a jasper stone, as the revelation of Jesus Christ. Jesus Christ is the glory of God and his glory came from the word which was in the beginning with God. John 1:1-14 tells us the process to the glory of God which begins with the Word and ends with the new beginning which is the Word made flesh. The glory of God is a revelation of the Word that causes Jesus to manifest.

And when you get a revelation of the Word that causes Jesus to manifest, he gives you a revelation of you. And Upon this Rock – *Stone* - does he build his church. (Matt 16:13-18) *Thou art the Christ.........thou are Peter............and upon this rock I will build my church.* Therefore the first thing the church needs is a revelation of the Word that causes the manifestation of the glory of God - the revelation of Jesus Christ. This is simply saying that everything that we see in the glorified church must come from the Word. In the Church we must get back to the Word and allow the Word to manifest whatever we've believed for. If we don't get it through the Word and faith we don't need it. If God didn't say it, I don't want to hear it. If God didn't give it, I don't want it. The glory of God comes from the Word of God that has been spoken again and again and again until the Word is made flesh and dwells among us.

So the new church is a CITY that's full of the GLORY OF GOD. It's a city that's full of things that have come forth through the word of God and prayer.

Rebuilding the Walls in Our Cities – City Prayer Watches

Rev 21:12 and had a wall great and high,

2. The Wall that was great and high represents the watchman and intercessors that birth that revelation throughout the congregation, and watch that everything that is supposed to be within is within and everything that's not supposed to be within is kept without. Watchman and intercessors are able to see what's creeping in the church, in the City that doesn't belong there, that didn't come from the Word.

The Greek word for wall is τίκτω tiktō, tik'-to, **wall g5088** *which means;*

> A strengthened from of a primary word τέκω tekō (which is used only as an alternate in certain tenses); **meaning to** *produce (from seed, as a mother, a plant, the earth, etc.), literal or figurative: - bear, be born, bring forth, be delivered, be in travail.*

Watchmen and intercessors take the Word and birth it in prayer and make sure that it is matured through a process of watering with the vision and purpose. Watchmen on the wall keep the Word of the church before the church and the vision of the church before the church in prayer, keeping out anything that is against the vision and contrary to the word.

199

Rebuilding the gates of our cities – city churches - And *had twelve gates,*

3. The Gates Of The City - Represents the Church of the city, which are the people, or the congregations of prayer in the city. It's the Greek word Pulon. From g4439; *a gateway, door way or a building or city*; by implication a *portal* or *vestibule:* - gate, porch.

> *Gen 28:16 and Jacob awaked out of his sleep, and he said, surely the lord is in this place; and I knew it not.*

> *Gen 28:17 and he was afraid, and said, how dreadful this place is! This is none other but the house of god, and this is the gate of heaven.*

When Jacob got a revelation of the house of God in Genesis 28:16 he said that it was an awesome place. He also said that it was none other than the house of God which is the gate of heaven. Therefore the gates represent the house of God, the gateway for heaven coming to earth.

12 City Congregations on Four Sides of Town – Gate Keepers

> *Rev. 21:12 And at the gates twelve angels, and names written thereon, which are the names of the twelve tribes of the children of Israel:*

> *Rev 21:13 on the east three gates; on the north three gates; on the south three gates; and on the west three gates.*

Now scripture in the Revelation says that this City Church had twelve gates, or twelve congregations. And at the gates, or congregations it had twelve angels, or pastors, and on the names of the twelve gates were the twelve tribes of Israel, which represent the city churches particular responsibilities in the city, as the twelve tribes of Israel each had a tow-post in Israel that they were responsible for. These 12 gates or congregations were three on four sides of town, each performing a particular function. And when they perform their particular function or responsibility the city is made new and filled with the glory of God. When they perform their responsibility there will be a new Columbus, or a new Kentucky, or a new Indiana, etc, as John saw a New Jerusalem.

**4. The Foundations - **Represent Apostolic oversight over the 12 congregations on the four sides of the City. The foundations of the city or congregations were in the walls, or they were in the watchmen and intercessors. And in them were the names of the twelve apostles of the lamb. This represent apostolic over-site being over and at the root of each congregation throughout the city that would be praying and correcting anything that was not right, and any congregation that was not fulfilling its particular responsibility or function in the city.

Rev 21:14 and the wall of the city had twelve foundations, and in them the names of the twelve apostles of the lamb.

Rev 21:15 and he that talked with me had a golden reed to measure the city, and the gates thereof, and the wall thereof.
Rev 21:16 and the city lieth foursquare, and the length is as large as the breadth: and he measured the city with the reed, twelve thousand furlongs.

201

The length and the breadth and the height of it are equal.

Rev 21:17 and he measured the wall thereof, an hundred and forty and four cubits, according to the measure of a man, that is, of the angel.

Rev 21:18 and the building of the wall of it was of jasper: and the city was pure gold, like unto clear glass.

Rev 21:19 and the foundations of the wall of the city were garnished with all manner of precious stones. The first foundation was jasper; the second, sapphire; the third, a chalcedony; the fourth, an emerald;

Rev 21:20 the fifth, sardonyx; the sixth, sardius; the seventh, chrysolite; the eighth, beryl; the ninth, a topaz; the tenth, a chrysoprasus; the eleventh, a jacinth; the twelfth, an amethyst.

Rev 21:21 and the twelve gates were twelve pearls; every several gate was of one pearl: and the street of the city was pure gold, as it were transparent glass.

Rev 21:22 and I saw no temple therein: for the lord god almighty and the lamb are the temple of it.

Rev 21:23 and the city had no need of the sun, neither of the moon, to shine in it: for the glory of god did lighten it, and the lamb is the light thereof.

Rev 21:24 and the nations of them which are saved shall walk in the light of it: and the kings of the earth do bring their glory and honour into it.

Rev 21:25 and the gates of it shall not be shut at all by day: for there shall be no night there.

Rev 21:26 and they shall bring the glory and honor of the nations into it.

Rev 21:27 and there shall in no wise enter into it anything that defileth, neither whatsoever worketh abomination, or maketh a lie: but they which are written in the lamb's book of life.

The Praying Church Network of Pastors & Leaders

City-Wide Corporate Prayer: It is the aim of *"The Praying Church Network of Pastors & Leaders"* to gather together as a City Church monthly for 24 hr Prayer Vigils to cover our city in Prayer and Worship, and to establish a culture of Prayer in the Churches in our City. In these monthly 24hr prayer vigils, Pastors, Church leaders, worshippers and musicians from through the city would each take a 2hr set in the 24hr prayer day in a designated prayer room in the city. During these 2 hour sets there will be times of worship, times of corporate intercession, and times of prophetic declarations spoken over a particular area of our city.

Through prayer and seeking the face of God together in our city **TPCN** will help facilitate this transition and expression of the Church in our city, to become a House of Prayer for all nations, and a City of Refuge for the oppressed, raising up a 24/7 covering and expression of Prayer and Worship, in the Spirit of the tabernacle of David.

Hope for Columbus Crusades: In addition to Prayer, *TPCN* will seek to host regular Justice Outreach Initiatives, called *Hope for Columbus Crusades*, aimed at releasing a breakthrough of God's presence and power throughout our city, working in relationship with the body of Christ to serve the Great Commission, as we seek to walk out the two great commandments to love God and people.

Feed My Sheep Food & Clothing Store: additionally, TPCN will establish a food & Clothing outlet store called, "Feed My Sheep food & Clothing store.

FMS would be operated exclusively and entirely by *The Network of Prayer Churches of Columbus.* Though the store would be set up just like a grocery store with quality food and clothes, with tags and prices on all items, the only prerequisite for Christian shoppers would be a weekly voucher received as a result of church attendance/membership with a church affiliated with Feed My Sheep food and clothing store. (*See the complete vision of FMS in the Hope for Columbus crusade manual, or in the book "My Money is Restored" on www.amazon.com*)

As a result of this Prayer Network and focus there will be the release of the Keys of David, to unlock the presence, power and provision of God over our region and realms of responsibility, establishing our city as a City of Refuge.

To read more on this focus; See *the Praying Church series* of books on *Prayer, Reconciliation* and the *End-times,*on www.amazon.com by typing my name "Brondon Mathis" in the search engine on their site.

CHAPTER 13

HOPE FOR COLUMBUS CRUSADE/FEED MY SHEEP FOOD STORE SET-UP MANUAL FOR CITY OUTREACHES

HOPE FOR COLUMBUS CRUSADES is an outreach ministry of the Network of Praying Churches of Columbus, aimed at preaching the gospel of Jesus Christ and His Kingdom in our city, through city wide tent services, as well as, bringing humanitarian aide and relief to the needy, undeveloped areas of our city.

OUR MISSION is to take the message and miracle of Jesus Christ from the church to the highways and hedges of our city, beginning with the inner city, helping the Body of Christ to fulfill the great commission to go ye into all the world and preach the Gospel.

THE NETWORK OF PRAYING CHURCHES OF COLUMBUS is committed and dedicated to replacing the crown of pride (Spirit of Leviathan) over the head of our city with the crown of His glory (Isaiah 28:3-6), establishing the Lordship of Jesus Christ over Columbus, Ohio. Within this mission we are dedicated to ministering the gospel to the poor and the least of these, as unto Jesus. Realizing that the anointing that destroys the yoke of pride in our city begins with the call to preach the gospel to the poor (Luke 4:18)

24/7 PRAYER AND WORSHIP MISSION BASES OF HOPE – Our Strategy is to target 4 inner-city neighborhoods within the city as the foundation for revival in our city, through Tent revival services on each side of town. These revivals will be followed up by raising up 24/7 Houses of Prayer and Worship Missions bases in the region where the tent services have operated, to begin restoring within these communities the Love for God and our neighbor.

205

Through Prayer and the discipleship ministry of Jesus Christ we will invade the communities of this city, rebuilding the old waste places and raising up the foundations of many generations, giving hope for the hopeless, and help for the helpless, *Putting the Neighbor back in the Hood.* Within these 4 H.O.P missions bases, 24/7 worship and prayer will go up continually to God day and night in the spirit of the tabernacle of David. Musicians and Worshippers/teams will play, worship and pray around the clock, hallowing God's name in earth as it is in Heaven. This will create an open heaven over our city, establishing Columbus Ohio as a city of Refuge. In addition to this, in these missions bases we will establish discipleship classes that will be offered, and benevolence help to be given in the areas of Drug and Alcohol recovery, Financial management, GED, Computer training, and English for Somalians, plus regular food and clothing distributions, car giveaways and housing and utilities assistance. Through this vision The Network of Praying Churches in Columbus will see thousands of lives transformed and restored to the Good Shepherd Jesus Christ.

HOPE FOR COLUMBUS CRUSADE DEPARTMENTAL VISION

Each department will list goals, purpose, and responsibilities for Captains and volunteers

Altar Workers

Goal: The altar team should be ready to receive those from the neighborhood with a welcome and the Love of God.

1 – The Altar workers should be prayed up as they arrive in order to help set the spirit under and around the tent

2 – During the service the workers will sit among the guests making observation to how the Lord is moving.

3 - At the Altar call the altar workers should encourage the guests around them to come forward by extending a personal invitation to go down to the altar together to pray the prayer of salvation or deliverance.

4 - At the time of the altar invitation, the altar workers should also be ready.

5 – The altar workers will pray with the guests who respond to the altar call as directed by the captains or from the stage.

6 - The candidates for Salvation will be taken from the altar to the salvation station where the guest will fill out the salvation decision cards and salvation packets

Items needed for this team

- Salvation decision cards
- Salvation Packets
- Pens/Pencils
- Arm bands

Crusade Schedule:

- *Meet for prayer and instructions – Thurs & Fri 5:00 p.m., Saturday 10:00 a.m.*
- *During and after service be ready to minister at the altar as directed*
- *Report to Food Distribution at the conclusion of the altar ministry*

Block Clean-Up

Goal: To present the love of God to the community by beautifying God's creation.

1 - Responsible for organizing and leading clean-up crews in the neighborhoods around the crusade location.
2 – Need volunteers to clean trash, mow, weed eat, paint, etc.

3 – The volunteers will enable those that are saved from the crusade to help clean up their neighborhood on Saturday 9:00 am –11:30 am.

Items needed for this team

- Gloves
- Trash bags
- Yard tools

Crusade Schedule:

- *Meet for prayer and instructions– Thurs & Fri 5:00 p.m., Saturday 10:00 a.m.*
- *Clean up neighborhood*

Children's Ministry

Goal: To provide an exciting Holy Ghost worship and fellowship experience for the children of the neighborhood.

1 - There will be a separate service for children on Saturday.

2 - This department will be responsible for putting together a children's service on Saturday.

3 - We will promote the children's service on Friday night to the parents at the service with flyers.

4 - We will meet to go into the neighborhood on Saturday to rally children for the service with incentives for children to attend.

5 - Captain will be responsible to secure all of the children's ministry items from the church for the children's service.

6 – Training Sessions will include Tuesday, August 22 and 29 at 7:00 pm

Items needed:

- Flyers for Children's ministry service time
- Flyers with incentives for attending the children's ministry service
- Children's Altar Cards
- Tables and chairs as needed
- Sign in forms
- Blow up rides with generator
- Carnival game equipment
- Other Children's ministry items from church.

Saturday Schedule:

- *Meet for prayer and instructions—Saturday 10:00 a.m.*
  - *Set up*
  - *Canvass neighborhood*
  - *Sign in and Free Play*
  - *Praise and Worship*
  - *Ministry / altar / sermon*
  - *Clean up*
  - *Carnival Games*

Clothing Distribution

Goal: We will be blessing the people with clothing.

1 - Clothing will be collected at the site and will need to be sorted before distribution beginning at 9:00 am on Saturday.
2 - Sort the clothing

- Remove all clothing that is not "straight and holy" such as dresses with spaghetti straps, mini skirts, etc.
- Clothes must not have any holes, discoloration, tears, bleach stains, etc. discard as needed
- Fold the sorted clothing department store style
- Box/hang the sorted clothing. Boxes will have labels of what type of clothing is in the box. Labels will be on all four sides and on top. Hang clothes according to type (ie: dresses/suites), gender and color. Hung up clothes are mainly dress clothes.
- Set out the clothes on tables. From left to right, categorize the clothing:
- Men's Women's Children Misc Shoes
- Put up signs that state what the clothes are (Men's, Women's, etc.)

- Captain is responsible for making sure all items needed are secured.

3 - Guidelines for clothing distribution:

- People will be allowed into the clothing area 10 persons at a time
- A team member will accompany each group into the clothing area
- There will be a time limit of 5 minutes for people to make their selections
- Limit 5 items per person

Items needed:

- **Grocery Bags and Boxes**
- **Clothes Hangers**
- **Suit and coat racks**
- **Tables**
- **Registration Sheets**

Saturday Schedule:

- *Meet for prayer and instructions 10:00 a.m.*
- ○ *Set up*
- ○ *Sort clothing*
- *Saturday after service distribute clothing*

Data Entry

Goal: Enter data from volunteer service and salvation commitments and report to the leadership.

1. Collect new Volunteer Data from Volunteer Registration Table & enter into (existing) volunteer database
2. Collect salvation cards from salvation station & enter into database
3. Enter food distribution flyers into database as they are collected
4. Give report of total volunteers, salvations, & families fed when each final count is tallied

Crusade Schedule:

- *Meet for prayer and instructions– Thurs & Fri 5:00 p.m., Saturday 10:00 a.m.*
- *Clean up neighborhood*

Parking Lot/Security

Parking Lot Attendants

Goal: Parking lot attendants are responsible the free and orderly flow of vehicle and pedestrian traffic in and around the crusade site.

1 – The attendants are responsible for directing traffic and parking.

2 – The attendants are also responsible for watching out for suspicious activity around cars (i.e.: people putting flyers on cars, vandalism, etc).

3 – The attendants will also make sure the pedestrians can walk and flow through the vehicle traffic safely.

Items needed:

- Cones
- Barricades
- Vests
- Flashlights

Schedule:

- *Meet for prayer and instructions– Thurs & Fri 5:00 p.m., Saturday 10:00 a.m.*
- *Park and facilitate traffic*
- *Meet for prayer and instructions*
- *Park and facilitate traffic*

Set-Up and Breakdown

Goal: This department makes sure that the equipment and grounds are ready for the crusade and are returned to their original state after the crusade.

1 - Volunteers will meet Thursday at 11:00 am at the sight to unload equipment, set up the tent area and stage.

2 - Pick up all trash and debris on site before unloading and setting up equipment.

3 – Help with cleanup and resetting of crusade area after the services.
4 - Breakdown of the tent and crusade site will begin Saturday after service once the area is cleared.
5 - Clean up area after breakdown of crusade site

Schedule:

- *Set up– Wed 12:00 p.m., Thurs & Fri 5:00 p.m., Saturday 9:00 a.m.*
- Conclusion of service for straightening and clean up
- After service for tear do

Food Distribution

Goal: Distribute food to the guests at the end of each service.

1 – 15 volunteers report to area for unloading, bagging and sit up at 1:00 pm on Thursday and Friday and at 8:00 am on Saturday.
2 – During the service the volunteers will sit among the guests to facilitate the flow of the anointing and assist the guests as needed
3 – At the conclusion of the service the volunteers will assume positions at the tables to help distribute the food
4 – Each guest will receive a portion of the food

Items needed:

- Bags
- Boxes
- TablesSigns

Schedule:

Meet for prayer and instructions and prepare food

Thursday 12:00-?, 5:00 p.m.

Friday 5:00 p.m.

Saturday 10:00 a.m.

After service distribute food

Greeter Ministry

Goal: The greeters should be ready to receive those from the neighborhood with a welcome and the love of God.

1 – Greeters are stationed outside of tent between tent and parking lot
2 – Greeters coordinate the volunteer sign-up table with badges and crusade information
3 – Greet guests as they come toward the tent
4 – Explain the program for the evening including clothes and food distribution, etc.
5 – The greeter releases the guest to an usher that seats them.
6 – During the service the greeters will sit among the guests to facilitate the flow of the anointing and assist the guests as needed
7 – After the service the greeters are to report to the food and clothing distribution center to help

Items needed:

- Water
- Badges
- Pens

Schedule:

- *Meet for prayer and instructions—Thurs & Fri 5:00 p.m., Saturday 10:00 a.m.*
- Before service greet people
- After service distribute food

Intercessory Prayer

Goal: The intercessors will under gird the planning and the crusade services in prayer.

1 - This department will pray before and during the crusade for salvation of the lost in the downtown area and for the flow of the Holy Spirit in the service.
2 - Before the crusade begins this team will prepare the grounds with prayer for the service.
3 - During the service teams will be positioned to pray behind the platform on the outside of the tent and at designated stations around the tent site

Schedule:

- *Meet for prayer and instructions —Thurs & Fri 5:00 p.m., Saturday 10:00 a.m.*
- After service distribute food
- Meet for prayer and instructions
- After service distribute food

216

Praise & Worship

Goal: Provide music for crusade services

1 – This department will provide praise & worship for Thurs, Fri, and Sat Crusade

2 – Responsible to gather praise & worship leader, front line/choir, and musicians used to usher people into the presence of God

3 – Provide hospitality and assistance to musical guests "Living Faith Mass Choir")ministering on Thursday night)

Schedule:

- Sound check – Thursday & Friday 6:00 p.m. (completed by 6:30 PM)
- Meet for prayer and instructions
- Canvass neighborhood

Publications

Goal: Responsible for the promotion of the crusade.

1 - Requires advertisements in newspapers, on TV, and radio.

2 - Oversee the production and printing of the artwork and flyers for the crusade.

3 - Determine feasibility of billboards, bus banners and other advertising mediums.

Schedule:

- On Facebook 6 weeks before Crusade
- On radio 6 weeks before Crusade

Salvation Station

Goal: the Salvation Station workers will process those guests who have prayed for salvation.

1 - The workers need to be ready to receive the candidates for Salvation as they are taken from the altar to the salvation station behind the altar on the right side.

2 – The worker will get the testimony on paper of each candidate for salvation

3 - The worker will hand them the salvation literature and answer any questions the candidate might have

4 – The worker will prepare the candidate for baptism in water if desired.

Items needed:

- Packets
- Towels
- Hose
- Water source
- Tank

- *Meet on site for prayer and instructions-Thurs & Fri 5:00 p.m., Saturday 10:00 a.m.*
- Before service greet people
- After service be at station/info table

Sound/Audio

Goal: The sound department ensures that the sound equipment is set-up and ready for the crusade, monitors the sound quality during the services, and oversees the breakdown of the equipment.

1 - This department will assist sound technicians in loading sound equipment Thursday morning at 10:00 am.

2 - Sound Captain is responsible for checking with sound man as to volunteer needs.

- *Setup*
- 6:30 pm sound check finished

TV Department

Goal: The TV department ensures that the necessary TV equipment is set-up and ready for

filming the crusade services and other ministry taking place on site

1 – This department will create TV Ads to air on Facebook & Youtube.
2—TV will film all ministry aspects of the crusade including services, food & clothing distribution, and Children's Ministry.
3 – TV Captain is responsible for checking with TV Crew for volunteers needed.

Schedule:
- *Setup*
- 6:30 pm sound check finished

Street Evangelism

Goal: The goal is to invite everyone in the community to attend the crusade

1 - Each member will be assigned to a team to distribute flyers and minister to the people in the neighborhood.
2 - Teams will canvass the neighborhood to pass out flyers and invite people to the crusade on Tuesday August 30th @ 6:30pm, Thursday September 1st @ 5:00pm, Friday September 2nd @ 5:00, and Saturday September 3rd @ 10:00 am.
3 - We will be passing out food and clothing flyers with applications attached encouraging people to bring them

back to the site to receive food on Thursday, Friday and Saturday.

4 - Captains are responsible for securing the items need with the administration team.

Items needed for this team

- Flyer advertising the crusade
- Flyer advertising food and clothing
- Tracks
- Salvation decision cards (Mission America)

Schedule:
- Canvassing Dates
  - Saturday, April 28th – 12pm
  - Saturday, May 5th – 12 pm
  - Mon & Tues, May 7th & 8th – 6:30 pm
  - Wednesday, May 9th, - 12pm
- Meet on site for prayer & instructions – Thurs & Friday 5:00 pm at site
- Saturday at 10:00 am

Transportation

Goal: To transport the volunteers and guests to the crusade site and to Hope City House of Prayer for services

1 – The volunteers will enable the buses to provide transportation for the crusade events both from the community and from other areas of Columbus

2 – Drivers will also be ready answer questions and provide information concerning transportation to the Sunday Hope Center services

Ushers/Security

Goal: The ushers will assist in making sure the service is peaceful without disturbance, the guests are seated properly and that the minister and altar workers are assisted in personal ministry during and after the service.

1. Lead the guest from the greeter to a seat under the tent making sure they are comfortable
2. Make sure the guest does not have any unanswered questions
3. Maintain order under the tent as the service time approaches
4. Facilitate the organized movement of guests during the altar service and give support to those who are ministering
5. This department will be required to be alert for those that would want to come under the tent but might feel apprehensive about entering in as well as keeping track of what is going on in the services.
6. Ushers 3, 4, 5, 6 are those assigned as "catchers" during the service. Other designated catchers will be assigned by the Service Director during the service. Each catcher is to stay within his designated area. The Service Director may change this set-up as required by the flow of the service.
7. Ushers 10, 11, 12, 13 are responsible for catching on the platform area. Be alert, be bold, do not hesitate. The Holy Spirit can move any time. These ushers are also assigned to line up those coming forward to the altar or platform. Number 12 will line up the left side; number 11 the right. A designated person will be assigned to line up the center.
8. Ushers 11, 12 will move down to the steps on their respective sides of the platform. (see Altar Plan.) They

should be ready to assist on the platform if called up by the Coordinator.

Ushers 7, 8, and 9 will come forward and stand in position ready to control the flow of people coming forward AND to pick up any that may have gone down under the power of the Holy Spirit. Always LISTEN for additional instructions from the pulpit or the Service Director.

9. The ushers should be alert to make sure there is no disorderly conduct during service, if there is, the ushers should be ready to escort those that cause commotion and confusion during the services outside the tent.

10. The captain is responsible for assembling the appropriate number of ushers to staff the tent services and the food and clothing giveaways after the services. (19 per service)

11. Head ushers will have radios to communicate with one another during services.

Head usher is responsible for securing items needed

Schedule:

• Meet at on site for prayer and instructions- Thurs & Fri 5:00 p.m., Saturday 10:00 a.m.

HOPE FOR OUR CITY VOLUNTER TRAINING CHECKLIST

1. CALL CRUSADE CAPTAINS TO MAKE SURE THEY'LL BE THERE AND THEY'RE READY FOR THEIR BREAKOUT SESSION
   1. Communicate times they need to be on site
   2. Communicate responsibilities
   3. Communicate Service Agenda (Brondon Mathis)

2. PRINT COLOR DEPARTMENT SIGNS FOR BREAKOUTS
3. MAKE SURE WE HAVE ENOUGH RESPONSIBILITY SHEETS FOR EACH BREAKOUT
4. PRINT INDIVIDUAL DEPT SIGN-UPS
5. REVAMP & PRINT COPIES OF SITE MAP W/DIRECTIONS ON THE BACK FROM HOUSE OF PRAYER
6. MAKE FLYER FOR PRAYER WALK & SEND TO PRINT SHOP
7. SECURE PROJECOTR
8. CONFIRM WE HAVE VIDEO FOR TONIGHT
9. FOLDER FOR ADMINISTRATOR AND ASST ADMINISTRATOR
   a. AGENDA
   b. DEPT OVERVIEW SHEET
   c. POWER POINT PRINT OUT
   d. ANY HANDOUTS
10. SECURE ITEMS NEEDED
    a. Dept Signs
    b. Dept Responsibilities
    c. Tape to hang signs
    d. Sign-ups for prayer walk
    e. Sign-ups for setting up the tent
    f. Sign-ups for Service booths for each breakout
    g. Copier
    h. Pens
    i. Site Map w/directions
    j. Power Point
    k. Video
    l. Projector
    m. Laptop
    n. Banner
    o. Power Point Print out

p. Copies of Food Dist Map included
w/Food Dist Responsibilities
q. Flyers – registration
r. Copy of Crusade Poster(s) ????
s. Video Camera

SITE MAP

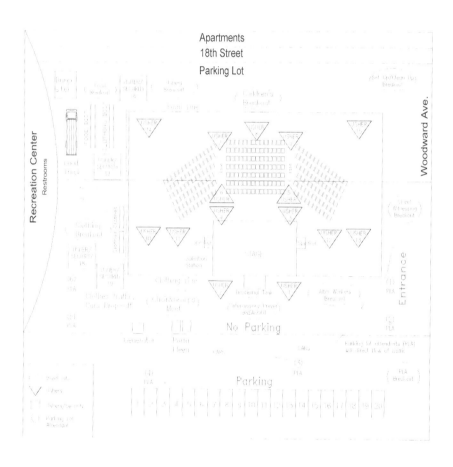

Feed My Sheep Food & Clothing Store is a vision of a food store that would be operated exclusively and entirely by *The Network of Praying Churches of Columbus*. Though the store would be set up just like a grocery store with quality food and clothes, with tags and prices on all items, the only prerequisite for Christian shoppers would be a weekly voucher received as a result of church attendance/membership with a church affiliated with Feed My Sheep Food and Clothing Store.

Unbelievers that would seek to shop at Feed My Sheep would notice heavily discounted prices in comparison to the worlds markets without compromising quality. Christian shoppers that would shop at FMS would be asked to simply give a donation. Our aim would be to provide for the needs of the body of Christ and the needy of the world by obeying Jesus' command to "FEED MY SHEEP" and to present the gospel of Jesus Christ to the world through the message and method of Love in action.

This will be accomplished by manifesting the compassion that Christ did when he fed the 5000 with the two fish and five loaves. It was this compassion that was instrumental in producing the miracle of the multiplication of the loaves and the fish. And it is this compassion that will be instrumental in providing miraculously for the needs, supplies and operational expenses of the body of Christ during the coming time of shortage of food in our nation, through Feed My Sheep. (FMS)

It is the aim of FMS to be a grocery /clothing store exclusively for those who are seeking to be set apart unto the kingdom of God, not just a food pantry or thrift store for the needy. The only prerequisite for shopping at FMS however will be Church attendance where the gospel of the kingdom is being preached. Shoppers will be able to receive vouchers from one of the daily/weekly services at the House of Prayer missions' bases in that city, or the other churches affiliated with the store throughout the city.

Those that do not attend a participating church will receive a voucher upon their initial visit to the store and a brochure with an invitation to the church nearest them. After that initial visit to FMS they will be required to attend a prayer/worship service to receive their next voucher to be able to shop at the store. If they haven't attended a service after their initial voucher visit they will be required to pay the prices that are listed on the items desired. Because our aim will be to have quality items, not just second hand stuff, we will be looking to draw the world from their conventional shopping/grocery stores to Feed My Sheep food & Clothing Store and eventually into the Kingdom of God through the message and method of love in action.

All ministries or social agencies that utilize the food and clothing store as a referral for their members will be required to pay a membership fee and become a monthly partner, donating monthly to the upkeep and operational expenses of the store. With this vision we will be positioned within the church, in neighborhoods and cities throughout to establish CITIES OF REFUGE, and POCKETS OF MERCY, during hard economic times coming to our nation and to the world at the end of the age.

Addendum
URBAN BELIEVER MAGAZINE ARTICLE OF A 2008 INNER-CITY REVIVAL:

PUTTING THE NEIGHBOR BACK IN THE HOOD

-FREE-

Urban

Believers

MAGAZINE

Summer 2007

Takin' it to the streets!
World Harvest Church's
Metro Harvest outreach ministry

The streets of inner city Columbus, Ohio and the newspaper headlines that often chronicle their stories, tell a tale Brondon Mathis knows all too well – Violence, Poverty, Drugs, Struggle, Defeat. It's not because he is one of the unemployed or poverty-stricken living in the nation's 15th largest city, but because he, and the outreach ministry he leads, wants change.

As the director of this inner city ministry, Mathis and his team of big-hearted volunteers have been on a relentless, four-year crusade to rewrite the headlines and inject hope back into the veins of inner city neighbourhoods by praying for the city every

230

day from 5am to 7am every morning, and all night every Friday Night from 11pm to 6am. The husband and father of five began his journey back to the streets of the city he grew up in four years ago carrying the 20-year-old vision of his pastor. Today his inner city ministry feeds, clothes, educates, and preaches salvation to residents in some of the city's roughest neighbourhoods through outreach services they call Hope Centers. They also host summertime crusades they call Hope for Columbus Crusades. And the tall, lanky church elder has his eye on doing even more.

In The Meantime, Ministry at the Three Hope Centers Continues.

On a humid Saturday afternoon in June a group of about 50 black t-shirt clad volunteers were busy turning hotdogs on a grill, tweaking the levels on the sound system and setting up chairs and tables outside the Beatty Recreation Center just southeast of Downtown. It was nearly time for another Hope Center Saturday service. With the music's bass thudding and meat cooking on the grill, the scene sounded and smelled like a backyard barbeque. Neighborhood kids ran back and forth between the recreation center's grassy courtyard and nearby playground equipment. It was going to be anything but church as usual.

Not long into the preparations Mathis appeared, taking long strides up the sidewalk toward the center. Like his volunteers he was dressed in the trademark black t-shirt. Also like his volunteers, he was ready to roll up his sleeves for the cause. About an hour before residents from the neighboring blocks began to trickle in, Mathis sat down with UBM to talk about the ministry's purpose and future. "The vision is to pick up the crown of the city and establish the Lordship of Jesus Christ. That's a vision God gave my Pastor 20 years ago," Mathis said, seated on the edge of the recreation center's empty auditorium stage. The idea was first birthed in a God-given vision in the Pastors heart to see the City reclaimed for Christ in 1984.

231

Psalms 144:13 is the basis for the ministry's outreach efforts. The scripture reads: "That our sheep may bring forth thousands in our streets."

Mathis Recalled the Dream as Vividly As If It Were His Own.

"He saw a big beast wearing (a) crown and the crown was shaped like the skyline of the city of Columbus. In the dream God gave Him a sword and he hit the beast three times at the knees and the beast fell and the crown fell off. The Lord asked Pastor who was strong enough, bold enough to pick up the crown of the city, which represents the authority of Columbus, and he said, 'We are.' That was back in the 80s," Mathis explained.

Like the coming together of pieces in a puzzle, it wasn't long before Mathis realized his part in that vision.

"After attending the Bible College at this ministry I got a desire to go back into the inner city to open up my father's church that we used to have back in the 90s," Mathis said. "I submitted (the idea) to the Pastor basically looking for his blessing to release me to go back."

Instead, his Pastor posed a question: "'Why don't you do (your ministry) from this church? I'll put you on staff, and send you back into the inner-city from this ministry,'" Mathis remembered his Pastor saying. Mathis accepted the challenge and the inner-city ministry was born. Because the ministry had yet to secure its own building, the first focus was street crusades.

"When we first started we started with a cookout crusade on Main and 18th. Our focus was that whole Main Street area." On a Saturday afternoon in September 2003 the ministry fed people, played music, danced, preached and offered an altar call.

"We had about 300 people get saved," Mathis remembered. "The burden was now how do we follow up with them. Our goal was to find a building that we could lease in that area and continue services. But we weren't able to find a building that was large enough for the people that were saved." In the face of obstacles, Mathis improvised.

"The first thing we began to do was develop teams to visit (those who got saved)," he said. "We would take vans and go into the Main Street area where the 300 had gotten saved and we would just go into their homes and disciple them and bring them to Church on Sundays." From there the teams helped create home-based discipleship classes throughout the Main Street area. The arrangement had its shortcomings, but Mathis and the volunteers continued the work.

"Since we didn't have a building, it limited our ability to continue to grow those individuals ... but we continued through the discipleship program and we began to really reach out." And the crusades continued. They held their first five-day crusade at Beatty Recreation Center in 2005. About 800 people received Christ over the course of the weeklong event, Mathis said. They developed a database to keep track of each person saved. "Basically the whole community came out and God moved greatly."

Mathis recalled an especially memorable crusade they held in a notoriously crime-ridden end of town on the city's Southeast Side known as the Maple Glen area.

"The COTA (Central Ohio Transit Authority) bus stopped going into the Maple Glen Apartments and the police were going in there because the buses were being shot at and they were shooting at the police cars," Mathis said, a tone of disbelief still lingering in his voice.

Despite cautions from police they decided to host a crusade there. The results were miraculous. "When we went in there and did our crusade, the people that were doing (the shooting) got saved." Mathis' said. He couldn't help but grin as he told the story. The owners of the apartment complex were more than grateful too, he added.

233

"They gave us a unit of 12 apartments and nine acres of land to build a Hope Center on. After our crusade many of the drug dealers and the alcoholics ... got saved. And the owners were like, 'If you guys can get these individuals off the streets of my complex and get them coming to church ... we want you in our community,'" Mathis remembered. *"And that's why they gave us the (apartment) unit."*

Subsequently, leaders at Beatty and another recreation facility named Barack embraced their vision and helped the ministry establish weekly service times after hours at their facilities.

Center Manager Anthony Dawkins helped them establish Thursday Hope Center services at Barack Recreation Center following outdoor crusades hosted there in 2007 just this past May. During the three-day event clothes and 40,000 pounds of food were given away, and healthcare and salon services were provided among other things. Dawkins remembered talking it over with his supervisor.

"I told him 'Wow that would be great if that inner-city ministry could come down here because a lot of these people out here don't have access to get to church because they don't have cars," Dawkins said during a phone interview. *"My supervisor is a believer and ... he was all for it ... I believed it was going to be something to meet the needs of a lot of the people."* *"I couldn't wait for them to come,"* Dawkins added excitedly. *"They come in such great numbers and it's so positive. They wouldn't let nothin' stop them,"* Dawkins said.

Barack and Beatty gave Mathis' ministry the perfect backdrop; the two centers are polished safe havens compared to the tangle of lower income neighborhoods that surround them. Today Beatty, Barack and Alum Crest High School open their doors one day each week to their outreach efforts. *"(The Hope Centers) is like a launching pad into the community as opposed to what we did on Main Street. Now every crusade we do we look to launch a Hope*

Center. Our vision is to reach out to the city – for God to save the city one neighborhood at a time." Mathis explained.

Moving beyond, the initial thrill and emotion of spiritual crusades, the ministry willingly enters the trenches with those struggling with lack in their personal and spiritual lives, to disciple them spirit, soul and body. Above all, they value the ministry of discipleship

"When people come here off the street often they need immediate help. Our first thrust is to feed them, clothe them, help them with their immediate housing needs, utility needs, family needs ... Anybody who comes into the ministry will get immediate help in the natural."

Among the other tools they offer at its Hope Centers are classes in job placement and interviewing skills, money management, A four-week class that teaches Bible basics to the newly saved, a six-month drug and alcohol recovery class, GED classes, computer training and more. They even give away cars to those who consistently attend and meet set criteria, Mathis added.

Before the classes, Mathis ministers the Word to those gathered there with a 30 to 40-minute service followed by an altar call. Later, during the classes meals are provided.

Like any church, the Hope Centers have their core of faithful members- mainly teens and mothers from the neighborhoods. About 30 to 50 people attend each of the centers regularly from the neighborhoods. Another 30 to 50 come every several weeks. Still, others linger on the fringes, coming only when they have *needs, all in all we average about 230 people per week per Hope center Mathis explained.*

"It's starting to take on the dynamics of its original intent as a neighborhood center of hope that operates as a community church with a service a particular day of the week, other than the service times at our main Church campus on the outskirts of Columbus, Mathis said. "Now, we still bring residents to the church on the outskirts of town on Sunday's and Wednesday's if they want to come, but more ministry is conducted here in the Hope Centers to minister to and disciple whole communities." We disciple residents to better their lives and to become more of what God has promised them," Mathis said.

The ministry is having a positive effect on the "churched" and the "unchurched," Mathis added. Recently a Columbus Judge ruled that as a part of a man's probation he had to attend the Beatty Hope Center every Saturday. The Beatty Hope Center is also on the court systems list of organizations they refer those that are sentenced to do community service.

Dawkins praised their efforts from his barrack rec. center into the Lincoln Park projects, to take God's love to the streets.

"Not only do they minister inside the building they have witnesses outside that will walk around (the neighborhood) talking to people, not trying to browbeat them with the Word, but just talking to them – asking them how they're feeling or do they know the Lord. You know, just something! Who knows maybe that will be a turning point in their life. If they just touch the life of one person that's major," said Dawkins. Mathis agreed. "I believe what the Church is missing today is the impact and influence in the neighborhoods that it used to have. (Today) you can have a church in the community and (its members) not know anybody in the community, nor look to try to find if there are

people in the community that need Christ. If the city is going to be impacted by the Church, every church has to have some type of influence right where they are.

Almost killed by the press,
entangled by the Spirit of this Age
But the BIRTH happened & although
the ~~struggle~~ wrestle to come alive was
a struggle, the chord was broken &
my Holy Spirit was present.

I am Jehovah Rophe
the God who so zo's you.
Come out from Among them
Be separate & Holy
Be Not entangled Again in the
yoke of bondage, Loosen up the
passage ways. Cry aloud, don't hold
back, I release you into Destiny
Catch your breath
        Awake! gain your substance
in me! Don't stop till you breath to Brown

coming out of
the Harlot
Babylon
&
This Antichrist
System

There is a great measure of
delirium

5/06/18

clev ⌐   5:31 p
col   │ cities of   refuge
cities ⌐

minute to spirit but
Body in Dsd to
come

Leviathan come out of her

Made in the USA
Charleston, SC
16 March 2016